KB104110

Unlocking the Power of Adaptation

How Our Minds Shape Language
to Fit the Unexpected

Eunjin Chun

Eunjin Chun

She is a psycholinguist and neurolinguist, as well as an author, whose expertise lies at the intersection of language and cognition. With a PhD in linguistics from the University of Florida, her research delves into the intricate realms of language comprehension, production, and learning, encompassing both socio-cognitive and neurophysiological perspectives.

Her passion for understanding the cognitive mechanisms of sentence processing spans first language (L1) and second language (L2) contexts. Her insights into (Second) Language Acquisition and Bilingualism/Multilingualism offer a comprehensive exploration of the dynamics shaping linguistic experiences. This book, rooted in her PhD dissertation, distills years of dedicated research into a concise exploration of these key areas.

By Eunjin Chun

UNLOCKING THE POWER OF ADAPTATION

How Our Minds Shape Language to Fit the Unexpected

Have you ever noticed how effortlessly you adjust your language when speaking to someone with a different accent or in a specific setting? These everyday experiences reflect a fascinating phenomenon known as linguistic adaptation, where our language processing abilities dynamically adapt to suit the current linguistic environment.

Consider a situation where you're conversing with a friend who just returned from a trip abroad. As they excitedly share their experiences, their sentences may reflect the grammar of the foreign language they encountered. Without even realizing it, your brain quickly adjusts to their altered way of speaking, allowing you to understand and respond easily (this is called "syntactic adaptation").

This book explores the intriguing concept of syntactic adaptation and how our brains seamlessly adjust to different language structures. This phenomenon is closely related to how our brains process sentences, interpret linguistic forms, and learn new language inputs, especially through implicit learning. Therefore, understanding syntactic adaptation can shed light on the underlying mechanisms of implicit learning as well.

Through in-depth psycholinguistic studies, we'll uncover the secrets behind this adaptation process. With real-life examples and cutting-edge research, we'll explore how our minds dynamically adapt to the ever-changing linguistic landscape we encounter daily.

A key aspect of this adaptation involves error-based learning theories. Our brains make predictions based on past language experiences, but when these predictions don't match the actual language input, we experience prediction errors. The magic happens when our minds adapt to these errors, fine-tuning our predictions to align with reality. We'll explore the role of prediction and how our prior linguistic experiences influence our ability to adapt during real-time conversations. These insights contribute significantly to our understanding of adaptation, especially within the framework of error-based learning theories.

Recent findings from linguistic prediction and priming studies provide compelling evidence for these theories, showing that language users predict upcoming information and are particularly sensitive to less frequent sentence structures. Interestingly, these structures, which induce larger prediction errors, play a crucial role in our adaptive language processing.

Psycholinguistic experiments offer valuable insights into how adaptation impacts our everyday communication. Whether it's understanding regional dialects or adjusting our speech to fit social contexts, our language processing is always adapting to ensure smooth interaction and comprehension.

This book, based on my dissertation studies, delves into the hidden workings of our adaptable minds and explores the profound impact of syntactic adaptation on our everyday language encounters. I invite you to join me on this captivating journey and be amazed at the remarkable flexibility and resilience of human language processing as we unlock the power of adaptation in our daily lives.

CONTENTS

INTRODUCTION

UNLOCKING THE POWER OF ADAPTATION

CHAPTER

01

In real-life language use, it is commonly observed that close friends begin to sound more alike as they continue to interact with each other and may also begin to use similar words or grammatical expressions. In addition, when people move to a new place, their language behaviors become more like those of people living in that place.

These linguistic phenomena are referred to as linguistic adaptation, a topic which has been widely investigated at various linguistic levels. For example, studies at the phonetic level have found that speakers quickly adjust to a speaker's accent (DeLong et al., 2005; Kraljic, Samuel, & Brennan, 2008); at the lexical level, interlocutors tend to use the same referring words (Brennan & Hanna, 2009); and at the syntactic level, speakers are more likely to reuse syntactic structures that they have recently encountered (Bock, 1986; Kaschak & Glenberg, 2004).

Understanding linguistic adaptation is important as it provides insight into language processing, change, and learning. First, since adaptation reflects changes in one's language processing as a function of exposure to certain linguistic input, understanding adaptation helps us to identify factors which can affect language processing. Elucidating these factors can provide useful information for communication improvement and language instructions. In addition, linguistic adaptation is related to how language changes over time through contact between speakers, including both diachronic language change (e.g., Middle English vs. Modern English) and synchronic variation (e.g., dialects).

Finally, repeated change in processing can lead to learning, and thus understanding adaptation helps us apprehend how language processing is connected to language learning. Change in linguistic knowledge through adaptation has been claimed to be a sort of implicit learning. For the case of adaptation at the syntactic level (Ferreira, Bock, Wilson, & Cohen, 2008), it is because change occurs regarding abstract rules (syntactic knowledge) without learners' awareness or explicit explanation of rules. Thus, learners cannot explicitly state the rules that they learned. If linguistic adaptation is related to language learning as claimed, studies on adaptation can contribute to the learning literature.

From a psycholinguistic point of view, it is also crucial to understand linguistic adaptation. Existence of this linguistic phenomenon requires theoretical accounts to explain its underlying mechanisms. As mentioned earlier, linguistic adaptation consists of changes in processing after exposure to certain linguistic input, which in turn may lead to learning, therefore, we need theoretical accounts unifying language processing and learning.

This study focuses on syntactic adaptation, namely, linguistic adaptation at the syntactic level. In this dissertation, what we mean by syntactic adaptation is change in language users' syntactic processing aligning with the current linguistic input after a certain amount of exposure to it, such as change in their preferred interpretation of a particular ambiguity after exposure to different types of interpretation.

Syntactic adaptation has been mainly explored using a priming paradigm in both comprehension and production. Such studies have consistently reported syntactic priming effects, that is, exposure to a specific structure increases the likelihood of reuse of the same structure or facilitates processing of a sentence with the same structure (See Pickering & Ferreira, 2008; Tooley & Traxler, 2010 for review). For example, when speakers are asked a question "At what time does your shop close?", they tend to answer "At five o'clock" whereas when they are asked the same question with a slightly different structure "What time does you shop close?", they are more likely to answer "Five o'clock" (Levelt & Kelter, 1982).

Researchers found an immediate effect of exposure to a structure on syntactic processing using a trial-to-trial priming paradigm, and long-term priming whose effect extends over longer period across several trials. Priming is also found to be cumulative as well; speakers are more likely to use that structure after cumulative exposure to a structure.

In order to explain findings from the priming literature, several accounts have been proposed thus far. They can be largely divided into two streams: accounts focusing on memory activation vs accounts focusing on implicit learning mechanisms. The former accounts hold that priming is due to the activation of recently processed syntactic representations (e.g., residual activation theory, Pickering & Branigan, 1998) while the latter accounts hold that priming is as a consequence of implicit learning (e.g., error-based learning accounts, Chang, Dell, & Bock, 2006; Change, Dell, Bock, & Griffin, 2000). The error-based implicit learning accounts, discussed in more detail in the next chapter, posit that priming occurs through prediction errors that speakers experience when their prediction based on prior linguistic experience mismatches with actual linguistic input.

Importantly, the recent literature on priming has provided evidence suggesting a relation between prediction and adaptation, in support of the error-based learning (EBL) accounts: greater priming or adaptation was observed for less frequent or less preferred structures (Ferreira, 2003; Kaschak, Kutta, & Jones, 2011; Scheepers, 2003; Wei, Dong, Boland, & Yuan, 2016). This inverse frequency/preference effect can be successfully explained under the EBL accounts: larger prediction errors experienced while processing less frequent/ preferred structures leads to greater priming. In addition, studies on prediction have found that native speakers tend to predict upcoming information using various cues in a given context such as semantic properties of verbs or grammatical gender (DeLong, Urbach, & Kutas, 2005; Kamide, Altmann, & Haywood, 2003; Szewczyk & Schriefers, 2013), providing indirect evidence supporting the EBL accounts which emphasize the role of prediction (via prediction errors) in adaptation.

The EBL accounts seem very appealing, providing a unifying account for change in language processing and language acquisition. In addition, as briefly explained above, studies on priming, adaptation and prediction report converging evidence for these accounts. Yet, the direct role of prediction in adaptation has not been explored, and thus little is known about whether adaptation is guided by making predictions, particularly, experiencing prediction errors. This study was designed to evaluate the EBL accounts by filling this gap.

The EBL accounts posit that language users make predictions based on prior experience such as parsing bias, and that they experience prediction errors when their predictions are not borne out. Crucially, these prediction errors lead them to change the connection weights in the linguistic processing/representational system, resulting in adaptation. In brief, the larger the prediction errors, the greater the adaptation. Then, it can be hypothesized that adaptation can be determined by prediction errors, presumably resulting from interactions between individuals' parsing bias and predictive ability. The magnitude of prediction errors may be affected by the interactions between one's predictive ability and the strength of their bias. In other words, those who have greater predictive ability and stronger bias can experience larger prediction errors and would show greater adaptation.

In this study, we defined prediction as generating anticipations about upcoming information at various linguistic levels (Dell & Chang, 2014, for more discussion, see DeLong, Troyer, & Kutas, 2014; Kuperberg & Jaeger, 2016) and tried to test the hypothesis that adaptation is guided by the interactions between predictive ability and parsing bias, presumably triggering prediction errors.

The results of our study suggest that listeners' bias and predictive ability help us estimate prediction errors that they would experience while processing less preferred structure but it is still not clear whether prediction errors lead to adaptation. The findings of this study advance our understanding of prediction (errors) and have implications for theoretical accounts of syntactic adaptation/priming.

This dissertation is organized as follows. The first part of the literature review (Chapter 2) has an overview of studies on syntactic adaptation (including syntactic priming) with a focus on important findings from prior research. Then, I critically compare different accounts of syntactic priming/adaptation. The final part of the literature review focuses on the potential relation between prediction and adaptation. In the methodology section, in Chapter 3, I introduce the norming studies performed to develop the experimental sentences used in the primary experiments; the materials and procedure for the online norming study are detailed. Subsequently, I introduce how the main study is conducted in Chapter 4, including the prediction phase (one visual world eye-tracking task) and adaptation phase (off-line pre- and post-tests with two visual world eye-tracking tasks). In the results section (Chapter 5), I present analyses of all data from each phase; analyses of eye-tracking data using mixed-effects models and of offline data (from pre-/post-tests) using logistic mixed-effects models. After that, in the discussion section (Chapter 6), I interpret the results and discuss implications of this research.

LITERATURE REVIEW

UNLOCKING THE POWER OF ADAPTATION

CHAPTER

02

Syntactic Adaptation

♦ ♦ ♦

During conversations, speakers adapt their language patterns (e.g., sounds, words, sentence structures, etc.) to align with their conversation partners. This linguistic phenomenon, so-called linguistic adaptation, has not only been observed in natural linguistic data (Schenkein, 1980) but also replicated in numerous experimental settings (Bock, 1986; Brennan & Hanna, 2009; Kaschak & Glenberg, 2004; Kraljic, Samuel, & Brennan, 2008). These studies provide converging evidence that language users constantly adjust their comprehension or production based on the properties of the language as used in its context.

More importantly, language users' adaptation to the current linguistic input seems to yield changes in their linguistic knowledge (Fraundorf & Jaeger, 2016; Kaschak & Glenberg, 2004). This linguistic phenomenon whereby speakers change language processing and representations in response to linguistic input and context is called "linguistic adaptation" (Chang et al., 2006).

Linguistic adaptation at the syntactic level (i.e., syntactic adaptation), which is the main topic of the current study, is defined as change in syntactic processing aligning with the current linguistic input. Over the past thirty years, syntactic adaptation has received a lot of attention due to its potential use as a window on syntactic processing for production and comprehension. Most of the studies on syntactic adaptation have used a priming paradigm that investigates how responses are influenced by preceding stimuli.

Accordingly, the priming literature has ample evidence of syntactic adaptation in production (Bock & Griffin, 2000; Branigan, Pickering, Stewart, & McLean, 2000) as well as in comprehension (e.g., Kim, Carbary, & Tanenhaus, 2014; Thothathiri & Snedeker, 2008; Tooley & Bock, 2014; Traxler, 2008). As the main purpose of this study is to investigate the role of prediction in adaptation in order to evaluate one of the theoretical accounts for syntactic adaptation (i.e., error-based learning), this chapter reviews previous research on syntactic adaptation, theoretical accounts for syntactic adaptation/ priming, and findings suggesting the potential relation between prediction and adaptation.

Syntactic Adaptation in Production

The first replication of syntactic adaptation in a lab setting was reported by Bock (1986). In her study using a priming paradigm, participants were instructed to describe pictures (targets) after listening to sentences (primes). After hearing passive sentences (e.g., *the church was struck by lightning*), speakers were more likely to use a passive construction than an active construction while describing pictures. In other words, speakers are more likely to use the same structure after exposure to a sentence with a particular structure. This is known as the syntactic or structural priming effect.

Syntactic priming has been well attested in many experimental studies; it has been observed across different types of structures and languages, among children and adult speakers, and in both written and oral modalities (See Pickering & Ferreira, 2008 for review). Researchers tested syntactic priming in various ways and reported important aspects of priming. Most studies have examined speakers' utterances (target) immediately after encountering a specific construction (prime). This way allows researchers to see the priming effect between individual prime and target sentences – known as immediate priming or trial-to-trial priming.

Such studies repeatedly found that speakers' syntactic choice for their utterances is influenced by the structure of the previous sentence. For example, speakers tend to repeat a prepositional object (PO) dative construction (e.g., *The boy gave a ball to the girl)* immediately after encountering it, relative to its alternative, a double object (DO) dative construction (e.g., *The boy gave the girl a ball*).

Trial-to-trial priming which reflects the immediate influence of a processed structure in a preceding sentence was found to extend over several sentences (Bock & Griffin, 2000). This long-lasting effect has been proposed to play an important role in language acquisition (e.g., Brooks & Tomasello, 1999; Savage, Lieven, Theakston, & Tomasello, 2003), and language change (e.g., Chang, 2008). Speakers' representations of a given structure can be strengthened through structural repetition (i.e., their tendency to repeat constructions), aiding the acquisition process (Tomasello, 2007), and ultimately yielding change in the probability of using the given construction (Chang, 2008).

To examine the potential role of syntactic priming in language acquisition, other studies focused on priming effects that accumulate across many sentences. These studies have found that speakers tend to produce sentences with a specific structure more often after encountering that structure over time. That is, the magnitude of priming increases over the course of an experiment with repeated exposure to the target structure. This priming, known as cumulative priming (Kaschak, 2007; Kaschak et al., 2006) is also found to last long, at least over a period of a week (Kaschak et al., 2011).

Additional important aspects of priming effects have been reported from production studies. First, priming effects are strengthened in case of lexical repetition across primes and targets. This is known as the lexical boost effect (Pickering & Branigan, 1998), and interestingly, this effect does not last long. Moreover, some studies have found a greater magnitude of priming for less preferred or infrequent structures than for preferred/ frequent ones - the inverse frequency effect (Bernolet & Hartsuiker, 2010; Jaeger & Snider, 2013; Scheepers, 2003).

Similarly, the priming effect interacts with surprisal, i.e., the difference between what is expected and what is observed. For example, each verb has its own bias, i.e., the tendency of a particular verb appearing in a particular structure. The verb 'throw' occurs more often in the prepositional object (PO) structure than in the double object (DO) structure, that is, 'throw' has a PO bias. Interestingly, the priming effect is greater when 'throw' (a PO biased verb) appears in the DO prime. In other words, greater priming is observed when a verb appears in a prime structure that is unusual for that verb (i.e., a prime sentence has high surprisal). This effect was corroborated by findings from corpus studies (Allen & Reber, 1980; Jaeger & Snider, 2008) as well as experimental studies (Bernolet & Hartsuiker, 2010).

Syntactic Adaptation in Comprehension

Similarly, syntactic adaptation has been observed in comprehension studies (see Tooley & Traxler, 2010 for review); the syntactic structure of a preceding sentence has been shown to influence the interpretation of a following ambiguous sentence. In addition, sentence processing is facilitated by exposure to a prime sentence with the same syntactic structure, evidenced as reduced reading time. In contrast to the robust priming in production, the priming effect in comprehension has been considered more elusive as some studies report lexically-independent priming effects (e.g., Kim, Carbary, & Tanenhaus, 2014; Thothathiri & Snedeker, 2008; Tooley & Bock, 2014; Traxler, 2008) but others do not (e.g., Arai, Van Gompel, & Scheepers, 2007; Branigan, Pickering, & McLean, 2005; Chen, Xu, Tan, Zhang, & Zhong, 2013; Ledoux, Traxler, & Swaab, 2007; Tooley, Traxler, & Swaab, 2009). As this study mainly deals with syntactic adaptation during comprehension, in the following section I will review the previous studies in comprehension in more detail.

Trial-to-trial priming

First, priming studies in comprehension reveal that processing a target sentence is eased after a prime sentence with the same syntactic structure or that interpretation of a target sentence is influenced by a prime structure. Such studies investigated priming effects using garden-path sentences which cause temporary parsing difficulty. For example, in a sentence-picture matching task, Pickering, McLean, and Branigan (2013) found that native English speakers' interpretation of an ambiguous prepositional phrase in a target sentence was aligned with a particular interpretation in a prime sentence.

At prime trials, participants were asked to match the correct picture to an ambiguous sentence like *The policeman is prodding the doctor with the gun*, when presented with two pictures - only one picture was matched with either the high- attachment interpretation (i.e., a policeman using a gun to prod the doctor) or the low- attachment interpretation (i.e., the doctor with the gun is prodded by the policeman) - and the other picture described the same action but with a different object (e.g., a policeman using a bat to prod the doctor for the given example sentence). At target trials, participants were again instructed to match the correct picture when presented with another ambiguous sentence and two pictures which correspond to high- and low- attachment interpretations.

In two experiments that manipulated lexical overlap (the same verbs across primes and targets) and lags (0~2 lags: prime-target pairs adjacent or separated by one or two fillers), participants showed a tendency to interpret a target sentence as high attachment after processing a high-attachment prime sentence regardless of lexical repetition or lags; both lexically-dependent and -independent priming effects persisted over intervening sentences, not decaying rapidly, though lexically-dependent priming was stronger than lexically-independent priming (note that lexically-dependent priming in production was stronger but did not last long).

Similar results were found in Kim et al.'s (2014) study using global attachment ambiguities (e.g., *The detective noticed the mirror on the wall with the crack*). In this study, participants read either a high-attachment prime (e.g., *The gardener watered the tree with the bird's nest with tangled roots*) or a low attachment prime (e.g., *The party took place at the house in the alley with the potholes*). Then, they were asked to answer a comprehension question (e.g., *What had a crack?*) by choosing either *the wall* or *the mirror* after reading a globally ambiguous target sentence (e.g., *The FBI agent noticed the mirror on the wall with the crack*). The results of reading time and target responses both revealed a priming effect; participants were more likely to reuse the primed structure when interpreting an ambiguous target sentence, and read a target sentence faster when they parse the target sentence using the prime structure.

In addition, priming effects in comprehension have been observed in online studies using eye-tracking while reading, eventrelated potentials (ERPs), and visual- world eye-tracking. For instance, Thothathiri and Snedeker (2008) employed a visual world paradigm which records language users' eye movements onto visual displays when they listen to sentences. Using dative constructions, they measured differences in looks to potential recipients and potential themes during an ambiguous interval which was created by using the same onset for the direct object noun in dative constructions (e.g., *Show the **hor**se the book* for the double object construction, *Show the **hor**n to the dog* for the prepositional object construction). Even though they used different verbs across primes and targets, participants showed more looks to the potential recipient after hearing double object constructions, but more looks to the potential theme after hearing prepositional object constructions.

Similar findings were observed in Traxler's (2008) study using an eye-tracking reading paradigm. More precisely, this study used sentences containing prepositional phrases (PP) which can be interpreted either as modifier-or as goal (e.g., *The vendor tossed the peanuts in the box into the crowd during the game)*. Comprehenders experience temporary ambiguity, namely, difficulty in processing the second PP (*into the crowd*), because the first PP (*in the box)* has already been interpreted as the goal.

Upon encountering the second PP (i.e., the disambiguating region), they reanalyze this interpretation by parsing the first PP as a modifier and the second PP as a goal. The reanalysis typically leads to an increase in reading times for the second PP. However, first-pass and regression-path reading times at the second PP were significantly reduced after processing sentences with the same structure (e.g., *The chemist poured the fluid in the beaker into the flask earlier*) than sentences with a different structure (e.g., *The chemist poured the fluid in the flask earlier*).

In other words, processing target sentences is facilitated after processing primes with the same syntactic structure. This facilitation effect has been reported in ERP studies (e.g., Tooley et al., 2009) in the form of reduced P600 effects. When reading reduced relative clauses (e.g., "*The defendant examined by the lawyer was unreliable*"), comprehenders initially interpret the verb *examined* as the main verb of this sentence, but this parsing should be revised as soon as they encounter the preposition *by*, which elicits a P600 effect. This P600 effect time-locked to the preposition *by* (i.e., the disambiguous region) in a target sentence was reduced when it was preceded by a sentence with the same syntactic structure, particularly in cases of lexical repetition (e.g., the initial verb).

Cumulative adaptation

More recently, studies using self-paced reading experiments report native English speakers' quick adaptation toward their less preferred or unfamiliar structures (Farmer, Brown, & Tanenhaus, 2013; Farmer, Fine, & Jaeger, 2011; Fine, Jaeger, Farmer, & Qian, 2013; Kaschak & Glenberg, 2004). For example, Fine et al. (2013) investigated whether language users' syntactic expectations change in response to repeated exposure to garden path sentences. Typically, reduced relative clauses (e.g., *The experienced soldiers warned about the dangers conducted the midnight raid*) are known to create garden path processing. The past participle (e.g., *warned*) triggers temporary ambiguity as this verb can occur as a main verb, or a verb in the relative clause.

Typically, native speakers of English prefer the main verb reading. Reading times for the disambiguating region (e.g., *conducted*) are therefore longer, relative to an unambiguous control sentence, when ambiguity is finally resolved as the passive participle is parsed as a part of relative clause. Because the verb *warned* occurs more often as a main verb than as a passive participle, participants in Fine et al.'s study showed longer reading times at the disambiguating region initially. However, the ambiguity effects became smaller as they had read more reduced relative clauses. This was interpreted as adaptation to the syntactic statistics of the current linguistic environment.

Interestingly, the readers' expectation adjustment for less frequent structures (i.e., relative clauses) was greater than for more frequent structures (main clause continuations), evidenced by reversed reading times for frequent vs. less frequent structures. That is, readers eventually showed a reversal of their parsing preference; after increased experience with reduced relatives, readers showed increase in reading times when the sentence continued as a main clause rather than a reduced relative (Farmer et al., 2011). This finding is parallel with the inverse frequency effect in priming studies (i.e., greater priming for less frequent or less preferred structures).

Furthermore, Kaschak and Glenberg (2004) showed that adult listeners quickly learn to comprehend a new syntactic structure (e.g., need + past participle). Their initial reading time for the new construction (e.g., *The meal needs cooked given that dinner is in an hour*) was slower than reading time for the standard construction (e.g., *The meal needs to be cooked given that dinner is in an hour*), but the processing difficulty for the new construction was attenuated very quickly (within 12 exposures to that construction).

More importantly, the adult listeners could generalize the newly learned construction to new verbs. Another study using self-paced reading experiments again revealed that readers are not only able to adapt to a newly-encountered dialectal structure (e.g., need + past participle), but to also generalize it to other structures that they may infrequently encounter (Fraundorf & Jaeger, 2016). In the first experiment, readers unfamiliar with this dialectal structure (i.e., participants from Colorado) initially showed slower reading for this structure (e.g., *The car needs washed*), but over the course of the experiment, they read it as fast as readers familiar with that structure (participants from Ohio, western Pennsylvania). In the second experiment, those who adapted to a newly- encountered dialectal structure (need + past participle) were found to generalize this structure to novel sentences (be-drop, e.g., The copier will recycled because it no longer works).

More fine-tuned adaptation, namely, talker-specific adaptation to syntactic structure has been reported as well. In a visual-world eye-tracking study using syntactically ambiguous relative clause sentences (e.g., *The uncle of the girl who will ride the motorbike/ carousel is from France*), Kamide (2012) found that listeners could adapt to individual talkers' structural preferences after exposure to utterances spoken by talkers who showed consistent attachment bias. They showed more anticipatory looks to *the motorbike* when they heard the talker who always resolved the relative clause to the high attachment (the uncle as the agent), but more anticipatory looks to *the carousel* when they heard the talker who always resolved the relative clause to the low attachment (the girl as the agent).

In a similar fashion, Kroczek and Gunter (2017) found speaker-specific syntactic adaptations over time (See Liu, Burchill, Tanenhaus, & Jaeger, 2017; Ryskin, Qi, Duff, & Brown-Schmidt, 2016; Ryskin et al., 2017 for different findings). In a within-subjects design, native German speakers were exposed to a speaker with a high probability (90.48%) of producing subject-initial structures (SOV speaker) or a speaker with a high probability (90.48%) of producing object-initial structures (OSV speaker). This exposure influenced participants' expectations for the syntactic structure of utterances spoken by a specific speaker; more assignments of SOV structure after listening to the SOV speaker but less assignments of SOV structure after listening to the OSV speaker.

This speaker-based syntactic adaptation remained until the following day, and more strikingly, even nine months later it could be rapidly reinstated with little exposure to the speaker-syntax coupling. Additionally, as SOV is the more preferred structure, greater adaptation was found for OSV structure (i.e., the inverse frequency effect).

In sum, syntactic adaptation has been observed in comprehension as well as production. These studies have shown that speakers alter their language processing in response to linguistic input, and potentially change their linguistic knowledge as well (though this aspect of adaptation is rather controversial in the literature). Indeed, readers showed rapid adaptation, after a short time of exposure, toward a structure that was previously unknown (Boland, de los Santos, Carranza, & Kaschak, 2015; Kaschak, 2006; Kaschak & Glenberg, 2004) and they generalized their adaptation to a newly- encountered structure to new sentences (Fraundorf & Jaeger, 2016; Kaschak & Glenberg, 2004). This change in speakers' linguistic processing and representations seems to occur without speakers' awareness, and to last long (Kaschak, Kutta & Schatschneider, 2011; Wells et al., 2009), suggesting that syntactic adaptation is linked to learning.

As syntactic adaptation including syntactic priming is closely related to language processing and learning, understanding the mechanisms of syntactic adaptation is extremely important to build a unifying theoretical account which can explain language processing, acquisition and change in language. Below, I will introduce the theoretical accounts for syntactic adaptation that have been proposed so far, and critically compare those accounts on the basis of previous findings. Understanding the current accounts is crucial as the goal of the present study is to evaluate one of these accounts (i.e., error- based implicit learning accounts).

Theoretical Accounts for Syntactic Priming/ Adaptation

◆ ◆ ◆

The current approaches for syntactic priming primarily focus on two mechanisms: memory activation and implicit learning mechanisms. These theories attempt to integrate important aspects of priming such as the lexical boost effect, long-term effect, cumulative effect, and the inverse frequency effect. Here, while comparing these accounts, I will point out how each account attempts to explain these effects.

Residual Activation Account

First and foremost, Pickering. and Branigan (1998) proposed that syntactic priming occurs due to residual activation of previous syntactic structures. This account is based on the findings from written priming studies in which participants showed a tendency to produce more double object (DO) constructions after DO prime completions than after prepositional object (PO) prime completions, and more PO completions after PO primes. The structural priming occurred in the condition where prime and target did not share verbs, but the priming effects increased when verbs were the same across primes and targets (the lexical boost effect). To explain these findings, Pickering and Branigan proposed the Residual Activation account under which the priming effects occur automatically regardless of other factors such as communicative goals or discourse factors.

According to the Residual Activation account, lexical entries in our mental lexicon, represented as nodes in Figure 2-1, are connected within a network. Then, the lemma node of a verb is linked to its combinatorial nodes which encode syntactic information about its potential combinations of arguments (i.e., the structure for a message). For example, the verb node 'give' is connected to two combinatorial nodes representing DO structure (NP_NP) and PO structure (NP_PP). When one processes a sentence with the verb 'give' in a DO structure, the combinatorial node of DO would be activated. This activation does not disappear immediately, thus it can be easily reused for the subsequent utterance.

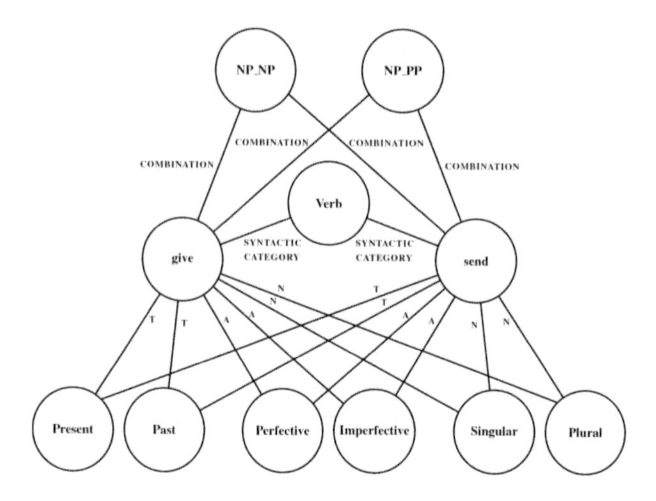

Figure 2-1. The representation of syntactic information associated with lexical nodes (verbs), T: tense, A: aspect, and N: number (Pickering and Branigan, 1998)

The priming effect can be explained by the residual activation of combinatorial nodes which is assumed to remain after use, taking advantage for the production of a subsequent sentence. In other words, the residual activation of combinatorial nodes can increase the likelihood of using the same combinatorial node for the subsequent sentence production. Since the combinatorial nodes (e.g., NP_NP or NP_PP) are shared between the nodes of the dative verbs, activating one combinatorial node (e.g., NP_NP) can lead to subsequent production of a sentence with the same combinatorial node (i.e., same structure) even when different dative verbs are used between prime and target.

Simply put, residual activation in combinatorial nodes increases the likelihood of using the same structure, resulting in syntactic priming, regardless of lexical repetition. However, residual activation between the links can further increase the activation in combinatorial nodes in case of lexical repetition (i.e., additional activation of the lemma node when the same lexical items such as verbs are repeated between prime and target), resulting in a greater priming effect. This way, the Residual Activation account successfully explains the lexical boost effect.

To summarize, the Residual Activation account explains both lexically independent priming and the lexical boost using transient activation of particular nodes in memory. As activation changes in memory are believed to decay quickly, this mechanism predicts that syntactic priming should not last long. However, contrary to this prediction, Bock and Griffin (2000; Hartsuiker, Bernolet, Schoonbaert, Speybroeck, & Vanderelst, 2008) found that lexically independent priming effects can persist across neutral sentences. In this study, they manipulated the number of intervening sentences (i.e., lags) between primes and targets (e.g., transitive and dative structures) to explore the longevity of syntactic priming. The results of this study revealed that priming effects over 10 intervening sentences were as robust as immediate priming effects (i.e., no intervening sentences between prime and target). The residual activation account does not include any obvious explanation for this long-lasting priming. There were no explanations about cumulative priming, the inverse frequency effect, and the surprisal effect.

Dual Mechanism Accounts

Hartsuiker et al. (2008) found that the longevity of priming effect differs based on whether priming is lexically dependent or not. In studies consisting of spoken and written production tasks, they manipulated intervening sentences and lexical repetition between primes and targets and found that lexically independent syntactic priming persisted over six intervening sentences regardless of modalities, but lexically dependent priming (lexical boost effect) disappeared quickly. They interpreted the difference between two priming effects as suggesting that a separate mechanism is responsible for each priming effect: an activation-based mechanism for short-term priming and an implicit-learning mechanism for long-term priming.

Similarly, Tooley and Traxler (2010) proposed the dual mechanism model, attributing lexically independent syntactic priming to an implicit learning mechanism, and lexically dependent priming (lexical boost effect) to short-lived residual activation (see Tooley & Traxler, 2018 for the dual mechanism model in comprehension). As shown in Figure 2-2, they proposed the residual activation mechanism which is very similar to Pickering and Branigan's. However, the residual activation in this mechanism is restricted to the link between the verb and the combinatorial node of the previously encountered structure (e.g., the thick line in Figure 2-2).

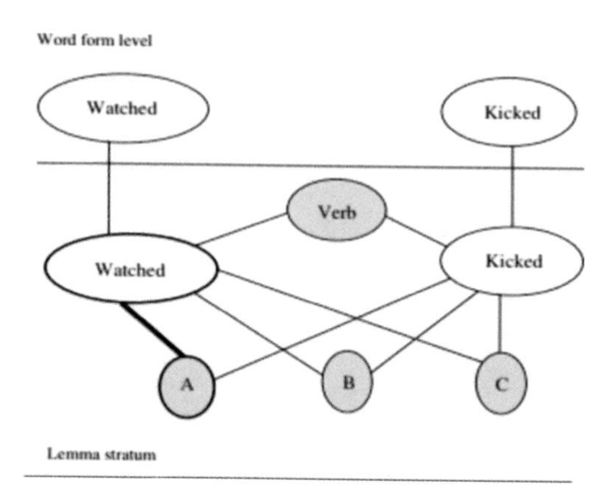

Figure 2-2. Modified residual activation mechanism (Tooley and Traxler, 2010)

This way, the dual mechanism account could predict the short-lived lexical boost effect as separate from long-lived syntactic priming. Crucially, however, these dual mechanism accounts proposed by Hartsuiker et al. (2008) and Tooley and Traxler (2010) did not elucidate other important aspects of priming effect, namely, the inverse frequency effect and the surprisal effect.

Another attempt for a more valid priming model has been made using general cognitive architecture, the ACT-R model (Anderson et al., 2004). Reitter, Keller, and Moore (2011) argued that priming can be better understood by modeling it as a combination of learning and spreading activation. This argument was in line with the view that "...a basic syntactic repetition effect may reflect the operation of a longer-lived, implicit learning mechanism, whereas in the short term, the binding of specific contents (lexical, semantic or thematic) and positions in specific structures triggers the repetition of structure" (Ferreira & Bock, 2006, p.1025).

The ACT-R model is based on a highly lexicalized syntactic theoretical account known as Combinatory Categorical Grammar (Steedman, 1999). In this model, chunks of lexical items are stored in declarative memory and compete for lexical or syntactic decision-making. Their activation can be realized through base-level activation or spreading activation. Base-level activation of a certain chunk is strengthened with each use of the chunk (i.e., retrieval) and learned over time. Spreading activation enables a chunk to be retrieved from declarative memory given cues in a buffer (serving as working memory). In other words, any chunk temporarily lingering in working memory after the utterance can serve as a cue to retrieve other chunks in long-term memory when there is any association between chunks (e.g., semantic association between *dog* and *cat*).

In the ACT-R model, base-level activation (a learning mechanism) is responsible for both long-term and short-term priming. Base-level activation correlates with retrieval probability of a chunk (i.e., the more highly a chunk is activated, the more likely the chunk is chosen), which provides a source for long-term priming (i.e., persistent priming over lags). This way, base-level activation enables speakers to acquire relative frequency (or preference) for CCG syntactic categories. However, the impact of a retrieval is stronger the more recent it is but decays over time. This can explain short- term priming. More crucially, Reitter et al. (2011) expanded this model using associative learning which can control the strength of spreading activation between chunks (e.g., semantic chunks in buffers used as cues for the retrieval of syntactic choices). The more associations between chunks in working memory and those in long-term memory, the stronger spreading activation.

As such, spreading-activation through this associative learning provides support for lexical boost effects. In addition, the ACT-R model explains how the priming effect interacts with frequency (i.e., the inverse frequency effect) as it shows reduced learning for more frequently occurring chunks; learning is decreased with the strength of priming, resulting in greater priming for less frequent chunks (syntactic constructions).

In summary, the ACT-R model was proposed to incorporate short-and long-term priming effects considering the differences between these two. When priming is modeled as base-level learning, long-term priming occurs as the retrieval probability of syntactic categories in memory changes. This way, priming is also cumulative in this model even though the degree of cumulativity for each structure is dependent on its frequency. That is, learning is reduced for frequently occurring chunks, which results in weaker priming for frequent structures but greater priming for less frequent structures (i.e., inverse frequency effect). Therefore, this model explains a wide range of empirical properties of priming: duality of priming (long-term vs. short-term priming), the inverse frequency effect, and the lexical boost effect. However, the ACT-R model lacks explanation for more fine-grained surprisal effects (e.g., greater priming in case a verb appears in a prime structure that is unusual for that verb (Jaeger & Snider, 2013).

Implicit Learning Accounts

Priming literature has reported findings of persistent syntactic priming over several sentences (e.g., Bock & Griffin, 2000) or days (e.g., Kaschak et al., 2011), suggesting that learning has taken place. Another view of syntactic priming is therefore one which claims that syntactic priming is likely due to long-term implicit learning, namely, unconscious acquisition of abstract syntactic processing (or implicit learning of grammatical encoding) over time (Bock & Griffin, 2000; Chang et al., 2006).

For successful comprehension and production, language users should correctly map messages (ideas to be delivered) onto syntactic constructions (i.e., grammatical encoding). Once they process or experience certain linkings between messages and syntactic constructions, the grammatical encoding can be tuned to compute those linkings again. Implicit learning accounts suggest that syntactic priming reflects grammatical encoding process tuned through exposure to incidences (Bock, Dell, Chang, & Onishi, 2007). This learning of grammatical structure is considered to be implicit as it satisfies criteria for implicit learning: 1) it is about learning abstract rules or knowledge, 2) the rules cannot be explicitly stated by learners, 3) learning is not obtained by explicit explanation of rules (or testing explicit hypothesis) but rather by coincidental cognitive processing of relevant information (Ferreira et al., 2008).

Along this line, Chang et al. (2006) proposed a connectionist model, namely, the Dual Path Model to explain long-lasting priming in terms of error-based learning. Their Dual Path Model incorporated two processing pathways for sentence production and syntactic development (learning): a sequencing pathway determining the word order (i.e., dealing with abstract syntax) and a meaning pathway encoding intended message (i.e., event-semantic representations of words). The sequencing system, trained via a Simple Recurrent Network (SRN) and error-driven learning algorithm, could learn how to create structured sequences for different meanings.

In more detail, the Dual Path Model is set to predict upcoming words in a sentence, based on preceding words and prior linguistic context (using sequential constraints and message related information, e.g., a noun can be predicted after the determiner *the*). Prediction errors occur when the actual input disconfirms the prediction (i.e., mismatch between input and prediction). Then, this model uses the mismatch information (i.e., prediction errors) to adjust the pre-existing connection weights on representations to reduce future prediction errors.

The SRN is mainly responsible for learning associations between verbs and other internal nodes, and the implicit adjustment would be reflected in subsequent production. When applied to a prime in a prime-target pair, the model with an error-based learning mechanism uses the mismatch between prediction (i.e., what the model predicts) and the actual sentence (i.e., the given prime) as an error signal that triggers a change in connection weights on representations to reduce future prediction error rate. This change in the connection weights leads to a higher tendency to use the structure of the prime sentence (i.e., adaptation toward the recent linguistic input).

In short, Chang et al. (2006; 2012) posit that language users constantly predict upcoming words, as they parse sentences, based on their previous linguistic experience (including long-term bias and recently processed input). If their prediction does not match their actual linguistic input (prediction error), the language learning mechanism adjusts the weights for a given predicted word in order to minimize future prediction errors. In contrast to a residual activation account of priming, this error-based learning mechanism not only provides support for long-term priming but also explains inverse frequency/preference effects (Bernolet & Hartsuiker, 2010; Jaeger & Snider, 2013; Wei et al., 2016).

More prediction errors are expected while processing less frequent/preferred structures, which triggers a more drastic change in the connection weights of linguistic representations regarding those structures. In the same way, the error-based learning accounts explain verb-based surprisal effects using prediction errors. In the error-driven learning mechanism, verb bias is learned by updating representation based on frequency. Then, a verb in the least biased structure creates stronger prediction errors, which leads to larger changes in the weight, ultimately resulting in greater priming.

However, the implicit learning mechanism does not yet explain the lexical boost effect, which renders it unable to explain the full range of syntactic priming effects. As a result, a separate mechanism employing explicit memory was proposed. At the stage of planning a target sentence, the repeated lexical items can serve as a cue to memory and increase likelihood to use the same construction for the subsequent production. Since explicit memory for words rapidly decays, the lexical boost effect is not expected to last long. This prediction is consistent with previous findings that lexical enhancement in priming was found at lag 0 (i.e., immediate priming) but disappeared at longer lags whereas structural priming remained still regardless of the number of lags (Konopka & Bock, 2005).

Belief Updating Account

As an extension to the implicit learning accounts, Jaeger and Snider (2008) claimed that priming (i.e., syntactic adaptation) occurs as language users continue to change their expectations or beliefs for a syntactic structure based on recent input, particularly - responding to its statistical distribution in the current environment. Similar to error-based learning, they used the term 'prediction error' referring to the deviation between what is expected and what is observed; syntactic prediction error refers to how much language users' expectation about syntactic structures is violated during incremental language processing.

They assumed that language users change their processes to maximize utility. Unexpected structures have higher syntactic surprisal compatible to larger prediction errors, which propels language users to adjust syntactic expectations in order to reduce surprisal (parallel to minimizing prediction errors). When one begins to encounter a syntactic structure more often, one's expectancy about that structure would increase as well - the more encountered, the more expected (i.e., statistical distribution of a structure modulates expectancy of the structure). As speakers are sensitive to both prior long-term and recent experience with a structure, even initially unexpected structure with high surprisal can be more accessible and processed faster through repeated exposure to that structure (i.e., increased expectancy). This model considering context-dependent constraints on expectations can account for the cumulative priming effect (Jaeger & Snider, 2013) as well as surprisal effects based on verb constructional biases (e.g., greater priming effect when a PO-biased verb is presented in a DO prime, Jaeger & Snider, 2008).

Based on previous probabilistic models of expectation-based processing (e.g., Hale, 2001), Kleinschmidt, Fine and Jaeger (2012) modeled syntactic adaptation with cue combination. This belief updating account focused on modeling syntactic adaptation in comprehension (typically observed as a form of reduced reading times for initially non-preferred or less frequent structures). This account viewed syntactic adaptation as a process in which language users rapidly update their syntactic beliefs in the current context given statistics of structures and reliability of cues regarding structures.

Therefore, syntactic expectations (or beliefs) in this belief update model are determined by relevant cues and linguistic experience (both prior and recent experience) via conditional probability. For example, in a sentence containing a temporary syntactic ambiguity like *The lawyer acknowledged the judge…*, *the judge* can be parsed as the subject of a sentence complement (SC) clause or the direct object of the verb *acknowledged.* Syntactic expectations about SC completions can change depending on different cues (e.g., verb types or presence of the complementizer *that*; SC completions are more likely to come for some verbs than others and are more common with the complementizer *that*).

In short, syntactic adaptation in this model was explained to occur as language users incrementally adjust or update their representation of a probability distribution over syntactic structures using their (prior and recent) linguistic experience and given cues in the context. Importantly, this model suggests that cues can be weighted according to their reliability when multiple cues are available in a given context. That is, the more reliable, the more heavily weighted. For instance, if the complementizer *that* is considered a more reliable cue for a SC structure than verb types in the example sentence above, the complementizer can be more heavily weighted and thus used for updating language users' syntactic expectations about SC completions.

As for the lexical boost effect, this account focused on fast decaying aspects of priming when lexical items are repeated. When lexical items are clustered, comprehenders may be sensitive to the repetitions of the same lexical items and consider cues more than statistics of the current environment for updating syntactic expectations. This way, structural priming can be shortly boosted but decay fast in cases of lexical repetition.

In general, this model is in line with the assumption shared by many experience- based accounts of processing--language users constantly update their linguistic expectations for more efficient language processing (using new evidence from input through monitoring). Using the notion of statistical distributions and multiple cues, this model could successfully capture syntactic adaptation as updating syntactic expectations in the current linguistic context.

The Relation between Prediction and Adaptation

♦ ♦ ♦

As reviewed above, the literature on syntactic priming shows recent exposure to a syntactic structure facilitates processing of the same structure, suggesting that language users adapt toward the current linguistic input. This adaptation seems to be explained using changes in syntactic expectations, as evidenced by anticipatory eye- movements during language comprehension. In a visual world eye-tracking study, Thothathiri and Snedeker (2008) found that listeners make anticipatory looks aligning with the most recently encountered structure as they expect to hear it again. These findings imply that the most recently experienced structure affects comprehenders' expectations for upcoming syntactic structure.

Other studies have shown that comprehenders use not only the most recent experience with a structure, but their cumulative experience with the structure as well for changing syntactic expectations (Fine, Qian, Jaeger, & Jacobs, 2010; Kamide, 2012; Kaschak & Glenberg, 2004). For instance, comprehenders experience temporary processing difficulty at disambiguating regions when processing garden-path sentences. This processing difficulty depends on their cumulative experience regarding how expected a specific interpretation is given the preceding context (Jaeger & Snider, 2013). In self-paced reading experiments, Fine and Jaeger (2013) found that this processing difficulty can be quickly eased as comprehenders frequently encounter an initially unexpected parse in the current linguistic input (or environment); eventually the unexpected parse even became faster to process than the initially expected parse. All these findings suggest that language users continue to adapt their expectations (shaped by previous linguistic experiences) to match the current linguistic environment (e.g., the distribution of syntactic structures in an experiment) using recent experiences with syntactic structures.

Using Prediction Errors for Adaptation?

An important question, then, is how comprehenders know how much to adapt each time. Several researchers postulate prediction error as a source of information to determine how much to adapt (Chang et al., 2006; Jaeger & Snider, 2013). They argue as comprehenders experience more prediction errors, they need to adjust their syntactic expectations more; the larger the prediction error, the more need to adapt one's prior expectation. Thus, the degree of adaptation after exposure to a structure is explained as a function of prediction errors experienced during processing the prime.

This explanation was supported by Fine & Jaeger (2013)'s findings from reanalysis of Thothathiri and Snedeker (2008)' study; syntactic primes with larger prediction errors (defined as – *log p(structure|preceding context)* lead to bigger changes in expectations (measured by differences in anticipatory looks to between potential themes and recipients) for the following primes. Jaeger and Snider (2013) also found stronger priming in the case of primes with higher syntactic surprisal given the subcategorization bias of the prime's verb. This suggests that the strength of syntactic priming is associated with prediction error which is sensitive to cumulative prior experience as well as recent linguistic experience.

In a similar vein, inverse frequency/ preference effect from priming studies shed light onto the relation between prediction and adaptation. Less frequent or less preferred structures elicit greater priming than more frequent or preferred structures (Bock, 1986; Ferreira, 2003; Kaschak et al., 2011; Wei et al., 2016). For example, English passives, much less frequent than actives, elicited substantial syntactic priming whereas the more frequent actives do not (Bock, 1986). This finding has been consistently reported from studies in production and comprehension. This effect can be explained assuming that language users experience more prediction errors from less frequent or preferred structures, thus leading to greater priming. The inverse frequency/ preference effect provides evidence that structural priming is sensitive to prediction errors.

Taking into account this evidence as a whole, it is plausible that language users naturally develop sensitivity to prediction errors for efficient language processing as expectations based on previous experience can help deal with uncertainty during incremental parsing (Levy, 2008; Smith & Levy, 2008). The approach that explains adaptation focusing on prediction errors is the error-based learning account (Chang et al., 2006). Fundamentally, these error-based accounts assume that language users make predictions based on previous linguistic experience, and that prediction errors occur whenever their prediction is not borne out (i.e., mismatch between their prediction and actual linguistic input). Then, prediction errors ultimately cause implicit change in linguistic representations to reduce future prediction errors, resulting in adaptation. In short, according to these models, prediction plays a crucial role in adaptation - without predictive processing, language users may not be able to experience prediction errors which presumably trigger adaptation. The crucial role of prediction in language processing has been supported by recent findings from prediction studies; native speakers tend to predict upcoming linguistic information using various cues from the given context.

Evidence for Prediction in Language Processing

Prediction can facilitate language processing and make mental operations more efficient. It can also reduce ambiguity by narrowing down possible variants during incremental comprehension processing, which may reduce memory load (Huettig, 2015). Despite these potential benefits, the notion of prediction was not considered in traditional language processing accounts, presumably due to lack of online methods to test it. However, current studies provide increasing evidence for predictive processing, regardless of modality, in first language learners (e.g., Borovsky, Elman, & Fernald, 2012; Mani & Huettig, 2012) as well as adult native speakers (e.g., DeLong et al., 2005; Van Berkum, Brown, Zwitserlood, Kooijman, & Hagoort, 2005). In other words, native speakers tend to pre-activate upcoming linguistic input (Kutas & Federmeier, 2000) or anticipate what comes next in given contexts.

Most studies investigating prediction measured predictive processing using online methodologies such as EEG (electroencephalography), or eye-tracking during reading or listening (e.g., visual-world eye-tracking). In EEG studies, prediction regarding semantic information (i.e., predictive semantic processing) was measured as differences in amplitudes of the N400--a negative component peaking around 400ms post-stimulus which is known to be sensitive to semantic processing (See Kutas & Federmeier, 2011 for review).

In a study using a 'related anomaly' ERP paradigm, Federmeier and Kutas (1999) found pre-activation of semantic features during sentence processing. In their study, participants were presented with high- constraint sentences such as *They wanted to make the hotel look more like a tropical resort. So along the driveway, they planted rows of....* Then, N400 amplitudes were compared when these sentences were completed with 1) an expected word (e.g., *palms*), or 2) an unexpected word from the semantically same category (e.g., *pines*), or 3) an unexpected word from a semantically different category (e.g., *tulips*). The N400 amplitude to the expected word was the smallest; the N400 amplitude to unexpected word was attenuated when the word was semantically related to the expected word (e.g., *pines*) as compared to when the word was semantically unrelated (e.g., *tulips*), even though either ending was equally implausible. This finding was interpreted as suggesting that semantic information was pre-activated based on sentential context.

In addition, Delong, Urbach and Kutas (2005) measured ERPs while participants were reading a sentence (e.g., *The day was breezy so the boy went outside to fly a kite/an airplane....*) with constraints that can lead to expectations for a particular article +

noun combination (*a kite* or *an airplane*). When sentences were highly constrained leading to expectations for consonant-initial words, the amplitude of the N400 at *an* (unexpected) was greater than that of the N400 at the determiner *a* (expected). Delong et al. interpreted these results as suggesting that predictions occur even at the level of phonological form. When readers expect consonant-initial words to come, their phonological forms are pre-activated as well with the appropriate singular indefinite article *a*, following the phonological regularity in English (e.g., a + consonant initial words, an + vowel initial words). As a result, the violation of the phonological regularity (*a* was expected when *an* was shown) could elicit an N400 effect (but see Nieuwland et al., 2017 for different findings).

More evidence about predictive language processing comes from eye-tracking studies utilizing the visual world paradigm. In such studies, predictive processing is found as a form of anticipatory looks onto target items even before hearing target words. For instance, in a study manipulating selectional restrictions of sentential verbs, Altmann and Kamide (1999) found that listeners show greater anticipatory looks to the picture items that satisfy selectional restrictions of verbs. In more detail, when participants were presented with a visual display (containing a boy, a ball, a cake, a toy car, and a toy train), they showed more anticipatory looks to the edible object (e.g., cake) while listening to the verb *eat* relative to listening to the verb *move* in the sentences like *The boy will eat/move the cake*. Strikingly, the percentage of looks to the target picture (e.g., cake) was significantly different between two conditions (*eat* vs. *move*) as soon as they heard the verb even before hearing the target word *cake*.

In a similar way, other studies revealed that native speakers make predictions during language processing, without much effort or cost, based on various types of cues: world knowledge (Kamide et al., 2003; Van Berkum et al., 2005), prosody (Nakamura, Arai, & Mazuka, 2012), lexical cues (Altmann & Kamide, 1999; Boland, 2005), and morpho-syntactic cues (Dahan, Swingley, Tanenhaus, & Magnuson, 2000) different kinds of representation are found to be pre-activated such as orthographic representation (Laszlo & Federmeier, 2009) and semantic representation (Federmeier & Kutas, 1999).

Does Prediction Directly Influence Adaptation?

A wide range of findings from previous studies in syntactic priming and adaption seem to provide evidence supporting error-based learning accounts. Not only inverse frequency effects and verb-bias based surprisal effects but also long-term priming and cumulative priming are well explained through changes in weights of linguistic representations triggered by prediction errors. Moreover, the review above on native speakers' predictive processing provides further evidence that listeners and readers predict, which is supportive of these accounts. Yet, the following reasons still make us question the direct role of prediction in adaptation that the error-based learning accounts posit.

First of all, native speakers seem to predict, which plays an important role in language processing, but it does not necessarily mean that prediction is a fundamental aspect of language processing or learning. Prediction is highly efficient as it can facilitate language processing and bring benefits to communication in dialogue (Pickering & Garrod, 2007). Its role becomes more important for language processing in some linguistic contexts such as noisy communicative contexts or the times when interlocutors communicate under time constraints (Kleinschmidt & Jaeger, 2015).

However, there exist some doubts about the necessity of prediction in language processing and some researchers claim that prediction serves instead as a helping hand for language processing (Falk Huettig & Mani, 2016). It was also pointed out that prediction may require expensive processing costs (See Kaan, 2014 for further discussion). These claims all raise a question about the notion that prediction is always necessary in language processing and that prediction errors are used for adaption.

Second, it should be noted that most important findings from priming and adaptation could also be explained by other accounts. For example, the belief-updating account posits that adaptation occurs through updating beliefs or expectations about statistical distribution of syntactic structures taking into consideration reliability of cues regarding structures. As this account proposes that adaptation is the result of belief updating driven by 'surprisal' (i.e., the difference in belief before vs. after updating), prediction, in the sense of pre-activation of specific information, is not required in order for adaptation to occur. Rather, deviation between what is expected and what is observed is enough to guide language users' adaptation. Likewise, as the belief- updating accounts can explain major findings about adaptation phenomenon, without the notion of explicit anticipation of incorrect items (i.e., prediction errors), it still remains unclear whether prediction is necessary for adaptation.

Finally, experimental studies on prediction and adaptation (including structural priming) so far separately yielded indirect evidence in support of the error-based learning accounts. Yet, there is no study that explicitly investigates direct links between prediction and adaptation, namely whether language users adapt using prediction errors. Without testing this hypothesis of the error-based learning, it seems hard to accept the necessity of prediction for adaptation.

The Current Study

♦ ♦ ♦

With the aim of better understanding underlying mechanisms of syntactic adaptation, this study investigated the role of prediction in adaptation by testing the hypothesis based on the core assumptions of the error-based implicit learning accounts. If syntactic adaptation is due to error-based implicit learning, sensitivity to prediction error should be observed. Note that the error-based learning accounts posit that language users make predictions according to their previous linguistic experience (such as parsing bias) and adapt when they experience prediction errors. The strength of adaptation may be determined by degree of prediction errors given context-dependent predictions based on language users' previous and recent experience; larger prediction errors would yield greater adaptation.

More importantly, prediction error seems to be modulated by one's parsing bias (i.e., previous experience) interacting with their sensitivity to prediction (i.e., predictive ability). For example, larger prediction errors would be experienced when language users process less preferred structures, and the extent of prediction errors would be even larger as they have stronger bias and greater predictive abilities (i.e., interactions between predictive ability and bias). Thus, it can be hypothesized that adaptation is guided by prediction error resulting from interactions between individuals' predictive ability and their bias.

In order to test this hypothesis, we exposed participants to their preferred structures and less preferred structures and measured their ongoing adaptation during exposure to each type of structure, and offline adaptation as a function of exposure. Then, we investigated whether their online and offline adaptation to each type of structure is influenced by interactions between their parsing bias and predictive ability.

To observe predictions based on individuals' bias, we manipulated relative clause (RC) attachment in this study. Just like verb bias, language users are known to have different biases for RC attachment. For example, in a sentence like *Someone shot the servant of the actress who was on the balcony*, the RC can be either attached to the first noun phrase, NP1 (*the servant*; High Attachment) or to the second noun phrase, NP2 (*the actress*; Low Attachment). Though most native speakers of English are known to interpret this ambiguous RC as low attachment (Frazier & Clifton, 1996), this globally ambiguous structure allows individual variances; some interpret that it was *the servant* who was on the balcony as they prefer high attachment while others interpret that it was *the actress* who was on the balcony as they prefer low attachment.

Therefore, RC attachment bias shaped by their cumulative linguistic experience was operationalized as individuals' parsing bias in this study. The fact that resolving RC attachment can be strongly influenced by semantic constraints (Hwang, Lieberman, Goad, & White, 2011) makes this construction suitable for the current study as we can create two conditions: 1) the condition where semantic constraints align with listeners' parsing bias which allows us to observe whether listeners make predictions based on their bias, and 2) the condition where semantic constraints are against their bias which allows us to observe whether they experience prediction errors and use prediction errors for adaptation.

Previously, Kamide (2012) tested the possibility of using this construction for talker- based adaptation to syntactic structure and revealed that individual speakers have different biases about RC attachment and these biases are subject to adaptation as they was changed in response to recent experience with that construction.

Studies about prediction in language processing provide a foundation for testing explicit prediction and prediction error. The visual world paradigm--tracking listeners' eye movements while listening to sentences--introduces a valid measurement for prediction in the form of participant's anticipatory looks onto target items prior to hearing target words. Following this tradition in visual world paradigms, predictive ability or prediction in the current study was operationalized as anticipatory looks onto target items before hearing target words. Observation of listeners' anticipatory looks over time during exposure to a specific construction can reveal how they change their predictions as a result of adaptation to the current linguistic environment.

Therefore, online adaptation was operationalized as change in predictive eye movements over quartiles (which correspond to the number of preceding items seen of the same type), and offline adaptation would be the change in the percentage of low attachment interpretations at a post-test, administered after exposure to each attachment, compared to a pre-test: a post-test 1 after a block with preferred structures (low attachment), and a posttest 2 after a block with less preferred structures (high attachment).

More specifically, utilizing RC attachment bias, we designed two phases of eye tracking experiments to investigate the role of prediction in adaptation; a prediction phase and an adaptation phase. A brief summary of these two phases follows (see figure 4-1 for the flow of the entire experiment).

The prediction phase

We measured participants' predictive sensitivity while they listened to sentences with RC attachment in which semantic properties of verbs serve as predictive cues (e.g., I meet the father of the boy that will ride/need the bike). We could quantify individuals' predictive sensitivity using their anticipatory looks on the bike during a target region (verb + the) between two verb conditions (biasing drink vs. neutral move).

The adaptation phase

Pre-test

we first administered a pre-test to identify participants' initial bias in RC attachment using ambiguous RC sentences. For example, after listening to an ambiguous RC sentence (e.g., Michelle sees the child of the mother that is talking to the woman), they were asked to choose an answer to a question (e.g.,

Who is talking to the woman?) by selecting either the child or the mother. The percentage of their LA interpretation was calculated.

LA block

Subsequently, participants with LA bias, measured by the pre-test, were exposed to sentences with their preferred structure, LA, in the first block (e.g., *I see the cat of the woman that will wear the shoes*; *shoes* as a target and *collar* as a competitor). Participants' online adaptation was measured via the change in their anticipatory eye movements over the course of quartiles.

Post-test 1

Any change in participants' attachment bias after exposure to the LA block was measured using post-test 1 in the same way as the pre-test.

HA block

Participants were exposed to sentences with their less preferred structure, HA, in the second block (e.g., *I see the cat of the woman that will wear the collar*; *collar* as a target and *shoes* as a competitor). Participants' online adaptation was measured via the change in their anticipatory eye movements over time just like the first block.

Post-test 2

Any change in participants' bias as a function of exposure to the HA block was measured via a post-test 2 using ambiguous RC sentences in the same way as the pre-test and the post-test 1.

It is important to note that predictive cues in the adaptation phase (semantic associations between subject and verb + semantic properties of verbs) were similar but somewhat extended compared to predictive cues in the prediction phase (semantic properties of verbs). This was to test whether language users' abilities to use a certain predictive cue could be extended to other similar predictive cues (i.e., generalizability of individuals' predictive ability). Furthermore, this operation enabled anticipatory looks on the targets in each phase to be used for different measurements (i.e., measurement for predictive ability in the prediction phase and measurement for online adaptation in adaptation phase).

Under the error-based learning accounts, prediction plays a fundamental role in adaptation since adaptation is claimed to only occur in cases of prediction errors (i.e., prediction mismatches the actual input) which are presumably triggered by the interactions between predictive ability and bias. Therefore, we tried to understand the role of prediction in adaptation by testing the hypothesis - derived from the EBL accounts - that adaptation is guided by prediction error, supposedly resulting from interactions between predictive ability and parsing bias. Based on this hypothesis, we made three predictions expanded below.

Prediction 1

In the off-line post-tests (compared to the pre-test), listeners with LA bias would show greater adaptation toward their less preferred structure, HA sentences. This pattern is particularly expected from those who have stronger LA bias and greater predictive ability, as they would experience the largest prediction error while processing sentences with HA.

Prediction 2

In the LA block during exposure to their preferred structure, listeners would show more anticipatory looks onto the targets aligning with their LA attachment bias as they are assumed to make predictions based on their bias. For example, those with LA bias would show more anticipatory looks onto the shoes than the collar as they process sentences with LA (e.g., I see the cat of the woman that will wear the shoes). As listeners have greater predictive ability and stronger LA bias, they would show more anticipatory looks to the targets at earlier times, and this pattern would be the same over time as they rarely experience prediction errors in the LA block. On the other hand, listeners with weaker LA bias and greater predictive ability may increase their looks on the targets over time as they repeatedly encounter LA sentences in this block; their recent experience with LA sentences can strengthen their LA bias and help them to predict based on it.

Prediction 3

In the HA block, during exposure to their less preferred structure, listeners with LA bias would show more anticipatory looks onto the competitors at the beginning of the block as they are expected to predict based on their LA bias and the prior experience with LA structures in block 1. However, over time as they adapt to their less preferred structure, their anticipatory looks on the targets would increase. For example, while listening to HA sentences, (e.g., *I see the cat of the woman that will wear the collar)*, those with LA bias would initially show more anticipatory looks onto *the shoes* (a competitor) than *the collar* (a target) as they would predict based on their LA bias (something that is likely to be worn by the cat). This predictive processing would lead them to experience prediction errors - what they hear (i.e., *the collar*) would be different from what they predict (i.e., *the shoes*). If these prediction errors are used for adaptation, they would change their prediction pattern over the course of the block, and eventually show more anticipatory looks onto targets. Again, this pattern would be stronger for those who have larger predictive ability and stronger LA bias (i.e., interaction effects between bias and predictive ability) because they would experience larger prediction errors.

NORMING STUDY

UNLOCKING THE POWER OF ADAPTATION

CHAPTER

03

In the main experiment consisting of the prediction and the adaptation phases, we aimed to investigate participants' online language processing by tracking their eye movements on visual displays while they were listening to auditory sentences (i.e., visual world paradigm). Thus, we needed pictures accompanied by sentences for experimental materials. Based off of Kamide (2012)'s materials, we created materials by manipulating semantic constraints for each task: the semantic properties of the verbs for the prediction task and the semantic association between the agent, verb and theme for the adaptation tasks. After creating the materials, we conducted a norming study to ensure that semantic constraints were appropriately manipulated for each task.

Method

◆ ◆ ◆

Participants

One hundred one native English speakers (43 women), with an average age of 33.5 (SD= 9.1, age range: 21~61), were recruited through Amazon's Mechanical Turk labor crowdsourcing service. We screened participants using a question about their first language (L1) before the task and prevented speakers whose L1 is not English from doing the main task. We further check their nativeness using the questionnaire about language background. Each participant received $1.00 in compensation for their participation. They all participated in this study after agreeing to an IRB approved informed consent form (IRB201602433).

Materials

For the prediction task of the main experiment, we created sentences like *I see the boy of the mother that will drink/ drop the milk*, using a biasing verb for the semantically biasing condition (e.g., *drink*) and a non-biasing verb in the neutral condition (e.g., *drop*). Participants' predictive ability in the main study was to be measured by comparing their anticipatory looks onto the target items in the semantically biasing condition with those in the neutral condition.

First, we created sixteen scenes for the prediction task, each consisting of two potential agents and three potential themes (See Figure 3-1). Each scene was used for two different verb conditions: in the semantically biasing condition, only one item in the picture (e.g., milk) had a strong semantic association with the verb (e.g. *drink)* while in the neutral condition all three items could be potential themes of the verb (e.g. *drop*).

We needed to ensure that this semantic manipulation of the verbs in each condition was not influenced by the potential agents displayed in the picture. To control for the semantic association between the agent and the verb, each verb was tested with both agents (e.g., *the boy* and *the mother* in Figure 3-1), resulting in sixteen scenes accompanied with 64 sentence fragments. A scene was accompanied with 4 different sentence fragments: 2 sentence fragments from the semantically biasing condition with each potential agent (e.g., *The boy will drink_*, and *The mother will drink____*), and 2 sentence fragments from the neutral condition with each potential agent (e.g., *The boy will drop_________*, and *The mother will drop________*). We created 4 lists of 16 sentence fragments (the same 16 scenes for each list). Each participant saw one list of sentence fragments presented with 16 scenes.

Figure 3-1. An experimental trial in the prediction task

For the adaptation task, we created sentences like *I know the owner of the cat that will wear the shoes* for the high attachment block and *I know the owner of the cat that will wear the collar* for the low attachment block. Then, we created scenes with two potential agents and four potential themes (See Figure 3-2). Two different versions of each scene were created with the locations of the agents flipped, resulting in 30 scenes. Two verbs were used for each scene (e.g., *wear* and *eat* in Figure 3-2). Each verb had a semantic association with two of the objects: *wear* being applied to the shoes and the collar, and *eat* being applied to the lizard and the cake. Each agent was also semantically associated with two of the objects. For instance, the cat is much more likely to wear the collar and eat the lizard while the woman is more likely to wear the shoes and eat the cake. When the agent is the cat and the verb is *wear, the collar* is a target item and the other wearable item (e.g., *the shoes*) is a competitor (but this item is the target item for the other agent, *the woman*).

Each scene was used for the sentence fragments consisting of four agent-verb combinations. For instance, four sentence fragments were accompanied with the given scene (e.g., Figure 3-2). Each fragment was expected to be completed with a word (i.e., target) in the parenthesis;

1) The woman will eat the_____(the cake),
2) The cat will eat the _____(the lizard),

3) The woman will wear the _____(the shoes),

4) The cat will wear the_____(the collar).

This manipulation resulted in two lists of 30 sentence fragments accompanied with 30 scenes. All the sentence fragments for the norming study were latin-squared and randomly presented. The sections of the prediction and the adaptation were counterbalanced.

The owner will wear the

- 1
- 2
- 3
- 4

Figure 3-2. An experimental trial in the adaptation task

Procedure

The experiment was conducted through Qualtrics, a web-based questionnaire, embedded in Mechanical Turk. Participants were screened in the beginning to exclude nonnative English speakers; once they unclicked to indicate their nativeness, they were prevented from proceeding to the task. We also checked speakers' nativeness using questionnaire about their language background which was completed at the end of the study. After consenting, participants were presented with a single scene and a written sentence fragment on the screen for each trial. Then, they were instructed to complete the sentence fragments by selecting the number of the most appropriate object in the scene and proceed to the next trial at their own pace. Each participant completed 46 trials in total (16 trials from the prediction section and 30 trials from the adaptation section) and a series of questions about their language background.

Analysis

♦ ♦ ♦

Using a question about their first language before the task, we could analyze only native English speakers' data. We analyzed data from 101 native English speakers. By checking the proportion of selections for each object in each trial, we ensured that semantic constraint was well controlled for every task. In the prediction task, for instance, the proportion of responses selecting *milk* in our example would be greater than that of responses selecting *newspaper* or *banana* in the semantically biasing condition (*drink*), but similar to that of responses selecting two other items in the neutral verb condition (*drop*).

We reexamined some of the semantically biasing trials that showed greater proportions for a competitor or a distractor rather than the intended target response. The trials whose semantic association between the verb and the theme or the agent did not seem strong enough (due to various factors such as the context driven by visual display, gender bias, or the size of the items) were adjusted and retested in another norming study in a similar fashion.

For the second norming study, one hundred one native English speakers (32 women) completed sentence fragments in the same way as the first norming study (M = 33.2, SD = 9.4, age range: 19-66). The strength of the semantic association between an agent, a verb, and a theme was considered to pick for main experimental items. (See Appendix A for the materials and raw data of the norming study). Responses to the finally chosen sentences for the main experimental items were as follows. For the sentences in the prediction phase, 96% of the participants (SD = 4.24) completed sentences with the target items when biasing verbs were given whereas 42% of them (SD = 23.68) chose the target items when neutral verbs were given. For the sentences in the adaptation phase, 86% of the participants (SD = 13.16) chose the target items to complete the given sentences while only 11% of participants (SD = 12.36) used the competitor items.

MAIN EXPERIMENT

UNLOCKING THE POWER OF ADAPTATION

CHAPTER

04

The main experiment largely consisted of two phases: the prediction and the adaptation phases. The flow of the entire experiment is given below in Figure 4-1.

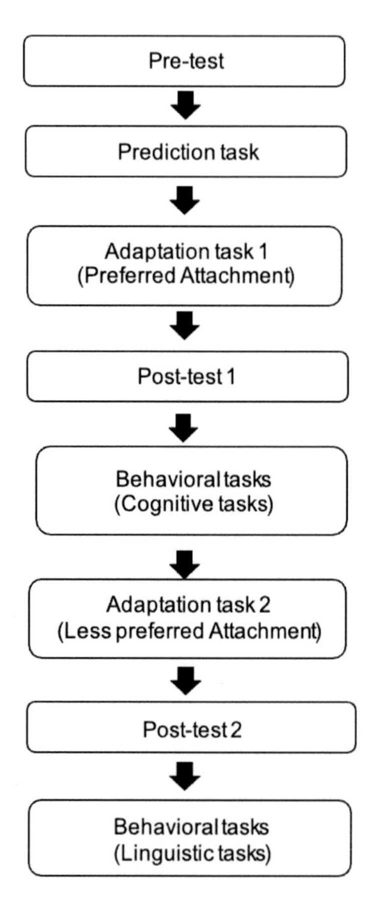

Figure 4-1. The flow of the entire experiment

Method

♦ ♦ ♦

The main experiment began with the pre-test that would identify a participant's RC attachment bias. Then, participants performed the prediction task. After that, they were asked to complete the adaptation task 1 which consisted of their preferred RC attachment in a block, and the post-test 1 which was aimed to test change in the participants' attachment bias after exposure to their preferred RC attachment in the adaptation task 1.

Next, participants were asked to complete the adaptation task 2 which consisted of their less preferred RC attachment in another block, and the post- test 2 which tested change in their attachment bias after exposure to their less preferred RC attachment in the adaptation task 2. Before the adaptation task 2, participants underwent a short battery of cognitive assessments.

These tasks were to separate the two experimental blocks. Then, after the post-test 2, they performed several language assessments and cognitive tasks. Finally, participants completed the LEAP-Q questionnaire (Marian, Blumenfeld, &

Kaushanskaya, 2007) which provided their demographic information including language background and education, and answered debriefing questions about the study.

Participants

Participants were recruited from various departments at the University of Florida. Sixty native speakers of English (functionally monolingual speakers), between 18 and 28 years of age (7 men, Mage = 19.9, SDage = 2.04), participated in this study for course credit or monetary compensation ($7.50 per hour). They had normal or corrected-to- normal vision, and normal hearing. None of them reported history of learning disorders. Before the experiment, they all completed an informed consent form approved by University of Florida's IRB (IRB201700448).

Prediction Phase

Materials

After the norming studies (see Chapter 3), we chose 28 experimental sentences (see Appendix B): 14 sentences for the semantically biasing condition (Biasing condition, henceforth) and 14 sentences for the semantically neutral condition (Neutral condition, henceforth). Fourteen scenes accompanied by 28 experimental sentences were prepared for use in a visual world paradigm experimental design. For each visual display as shown in Figure 4-2, two sentences (one for each condition) were prepared as follows: 1) *I meet the father of the boy that will ride the bike* (Biasing condition), and 2) *I meet the father of the boy that will need the bike* (Neutral condition). For fillers, we created 16 RC sentences (e.g., *The chef knows the girl that will cook the chicken*) which have only one possible referent, and 16 scenes to accompany them.

Figure 4–2. An example picture for the prediction task

All the experimental sentences were recorded by a female native English speaker using a Marantz PMD660 Digital Recorder. Each sentence was recorded using 16-bit stereo PCM sound at a sampling rate of 44.1 kHz with an external head mounted microphone. The speaker was asked to record each sentence 3 times, and then the best version was chosen based on speech rate and sound quality. We edited each audio file using Praat audio editing software (Boersma & Weenink, 2016), in order to get rid of any bias driven by prosodic cues (e.g., prosodic boundary and pitch accents). We first deleted any pauses 1) between NP1 (e.g., the father) and *of*, 2) between *of* and NP2 (e.g., *the boy*), and 3) between NP2 and *that*. Then, we manipulated the pitch of the two NPs to be equal in each sentence. We also equalized the duration of the target region (e.g., *verb + the*) using the mean duration of all the target regions. This was done to ensure that participants were given the same amount of time to use the semantic information of the verb to anticipate the target in each sentence.
Finally, we normalized all the sound files using the mean intensity (M = 74.91 dB). After editing the sound files, the naturalness of the resultant auditory stimuli was judged and confirmed by ten listeners who did not know the purpose of this study. Auditory stimuli, consisting of 28 experimental sentences intermixed with 16 filler sentences, were randomly presented via headphones.

Procedure

In a sound-attenuated room, participants were seated in a comfortable chair with a distance of 70 cm from a computer screen. They wore a head-mounted eye-tracker (Eyelink 2 version 2.21, SR research, Mississauga, Ontario, Canada), which was focused and calibrated. After camera setup, an automatic 9-point calibration and validation routine was performed using a standard black and white 20-point bull's-eye image. Visual stimuli were presented at a resolution of 1024x768 pixels using a PC computer running EyeLink Experiment Builder software (SR Research, Mississauga, Ontario, Canada) and auditory stimuli were presented by the same computer through head phones.

Eye movements were recorded at 500 Hz sampling rate. Participants were told that they would see pictures and listen to sentences, and that they would be asked to click on the last mentioned item in the display using a mouse. This was to encourage participants to move their eyes in response to the auditory stimuli. Before the main experiment, they were given 5 practice trials until they fully understood the task.

Each trial starts with a bull's-eye image in the center of the screen which participants were instructed to fixate on to proceed to the trial. This image served as a drift correction dot before each trial. Participants were shown a visual display for 2000ms before sentence onset for a preview (cf. Huettig, Rommers, & Meyer, 2011). The pictures remained on the screen after sentence offset until participants had clicked on the last mentioned item from the auditory stimulus (see Figure 4-3). The stimuli were presented in a random order. Recalibration of the eye-tracker was performed between trials only when it was required. This section of the study (prediction phase) lasted 15- 20 minutes.

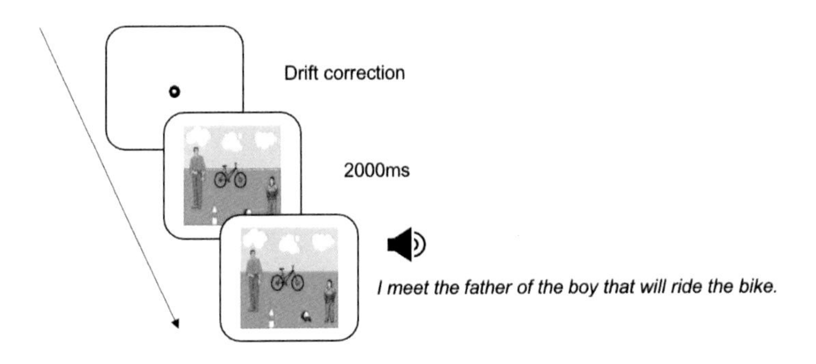

Figure 4-3. The flow of an experimental trial in the prediction task

Adaptation Phase

The adaptation phases consisted of pre- and post-tests, and adaptation tasks in two attachment blocks: a low attachment block and a high attachment block. It took about one hour to finish the entire section of the adaptation phases.

Materials

Offline adaptation tasks (pre-and post-tests)

Three sets of pre- and post- tests were prepared to determine individuals' attachment preference or bias. Each test consisted of 12 sentences containing a relative clause with ambiguous attachment (e.g., *Michelle sees the child of the mother that is talking to the woman;* See Appendix C for the experimental sentences in pre-and post-tests) and 16 fillers which contained a relative clause with one NP (e.g., *The banker sees the customer that is using the phone*). Three pre-and post-tests were counterbalanced across the participants, and the sentences in each test were pseudorandomized, with the fillers intermixed after one or two experimental sentences. In the pre-and post-tests, participants were asked to listen to each sentence and answer comprehension questions by pressing "1" or "2". The questions were asking whether relative clauses would be attached to the first NP or the second NP (e.g., *Who is talking to the woman?*). For the answer choices, half of "1" were matched with the NP1 (e.g., *the child)* and the other half of "1" were matched with the NP2 (e.g., *the mother*). The materials for the pre-and post-tests were recorded and manipulated in the same way (the mean intensity: 74.63 dB) as those for the prediction task.

Online adaptation tasks

For the adaptation task, we modified the materials of Kamide's (2012) study. By counterbalancing two NPs, we created two sets of 28 sentences containing RCs that are semantically more biased toward NP1 attachment (e.g., *I know the uncle of the girl that will ride the motorbike)* for the high attachment block, and another two sets of 28 sentences containing RCs that are semantically more biased toward NP2 attachment (e.g., *I see the uncle of the girl that will ride the rocking horse)* for the low attachment block.

For the Visual World Paradigm, we chose two sets of 14 scenes that would be presented with experimental sentences by switching the positions of two agents. Each scene (see Figure 4-4 for an example), containing two agents and four potential themes, was used for 4 experimental sentences: 1) *I know the uncle of the girl that will ride the motorbike,* 2) *That is the niece of the man that will ride the rocking horse,* 3) *I see the uncle of the girl that will blow the tuba, and 4) I know the niece of the man that will blow the pinwheel*. Again, all the sentences for the adaptation were recorded and manipulated in the same way (the mean intensity M = 74.83 dB) as those for the prediction task.

Figure 4-4. An example picture for the adaptation task

Procedure

Pre-test

After the instructions, participants listened to auditory sentences and answered comprehension questions about RC sentences with ambiguous attachment by pressing "1" or "2" which correspond to NP1 and NP2. The percentage of LA interpretations was calculated: the more percentage of low attachment interpretations, the more biased toward low attachment.

Online adaptation task 1 (Preferred attachment block)

In the adaptation task 1, participants were first exposed to sentences biased toward their preferred attachment. Fifty-six experimental sentences in the first block were aligned with their preference in RC attachment. Low attachers were exposed to the low attachment block in which all relative clauses are semantically biased toward the NP2 attachment (see Appendix D for the experimental sentences in the low attachment block).

On the other hand, those who prefer high attachment (scoring less than or equal to 5 low attachment interpretations at the pre-test) were exposed to the high attachment block in which all relative clauses are semantically biased toward the NP1 attachment. The adaptation task using the visual world paradigm was carried out in the same way as the prediction task. The only difference in procedures between the two tasks is that after listening to auditory sentences in the adaptation task, participants were asked to answer comprehension questions (e.g., *Who will ride the rocking horse?)* by pressing "Z" or "V" which correspond to NP1 and NP2. These comprehension questions were included to make participants engaged in the tasks and to check their RC attachment interpretations. Two thirds of the experimental trials were followed by comprehension questions, and the feedback of a sad face was shown only when their answers were not correct (see Figure 4-5).

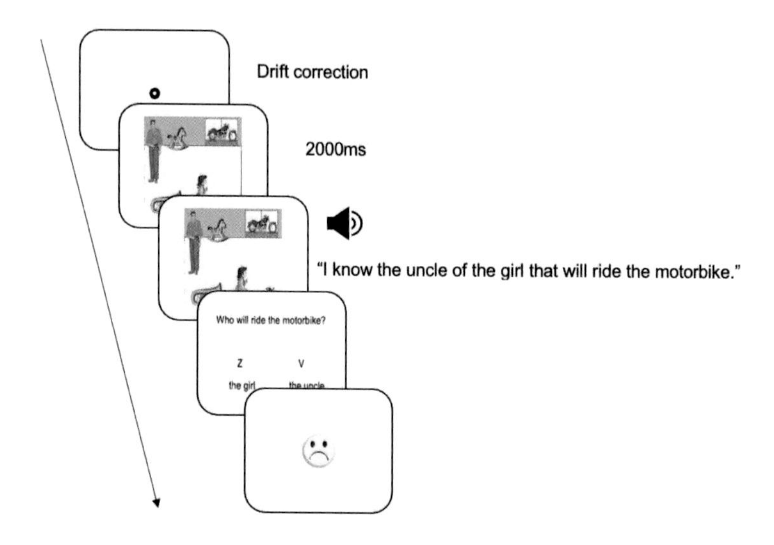

Figure 4-5. The flow of an experimental trial in the adaptation task

Post-test I

After the adaptation task 1, we administered the post-test 1 to measure participants' adaptation toward their preferred attachment. The procedure was the same as in the pre-test: after listening to auditory sentences, participants answered comprehension questions about ambiguous RC sentences by pressing "1" or "2".

Behavioral tasks

A battery of cognitive tasks was conducted shortly (approximately 10 minutes) to separate two blocks (Adaptation task 1 from Adaptation task 2). The tasks involved executive function tasks (e.g., Stroop task, Flanker task, and recalling letters) and digit span tasks in a forward and backward fashion. These tasks took approximately 20 minutes. As these tasks served as a distractor between experimental blocks, this data will not be explored in this study.

Online adaptation task 2 (Less preferred attachment block)

In the adaptation task 2, participants were exposed to sentences with their less preferred RC attachment. Thus, all 56 experimental sentences in this block had RC attachments that were against participants' preference in RC attachment, as determined by the initial pre- test. Low attachers were exposed to the high attachment block (see Appendix E for the experimental sentences in the HA block), whereas high attachers were exposed to the low attachment block. The adaptation task 2 was administered in the same way as the adaptation task 1.

Post-test 2

After exposure to their less preferred structures in the adaptation task 2, we measured participants' adaptation toward their less-preferred attachment through the post-test 2 in the same way with the pre-test and the post-test1.

Behavioral tasks

At the end, several behavioral tasks including cognitive tasks and linguistic tasks were administered using E-prime. They included Shipley Vocabulary Test, grammar and cloze section of the MELICET, and statistical learning task; however, these tasks are not directly related to the main research questions in this study and the data will not be reported in the analysis. Finally, participants completed the LEAP-Q (Marian et al., 2007) which provided their demographic information (e.g., age, country of origin) as well as language experience and proficiency. It took around 30 minutes to finish all the behavioral tasks and questionnaire.

ANALYSIS AND RESULTS

UNLOCKING THE POWER OF ADAPTATION

CHAPTER

05

We could not recruit enough participants with high attachment (HA) preference. Therefore, we analyzed the data from 44 native English speakers (8 men) who showed different degrees of low attachment (LA) preference (greater than 6 LA interpretations out of 12 ambiguous RC sentences), determined on the basis of the pre-test. Information about these participants is given in Table 5-1.

Table 5-1. Participant information

	Range	Mean	SD
Age	18-28	19.9	2.05
Digit Span Forward	4-12	9.20 (out of 12)	1.99
Digit Span Backward	3-11	7.50 (out of 12)	1.81
Shipley (Vocabulary)	25-40	31.53 (out of 40)	3.62
MELICET (Grammar)	36-49	45.10 (out of 50)	2.92

Prediction Phase

♦ ♦ ♦

The prediction phase was designed to measure individual participants' predictive ability. In this phase, participants were presented with visual displays and asked to click the last mentioned item after listening to auditory stimuli while their eye movements were being recorded. The clicking task was included not only to align their eye movements with language processing, but also to check whether they paid attention to the task. Listeners were expected to show anticipatory looks at target items before hearing target words if they make predictions using given cues. If so, we expected to quantify individuals' predictive ability using difference in their anticipatory looks on target items between two verb conditions (Biasing vs. Neutral).

Behavioral task accuracy

Mouse-clicking responses (i.e., clicking the last- mentioned items) showed a mean accuracy of 27.93 (out of 28 trials, SD=0.25) meaning that participants appropriately performed the task.

Eye-tracking data analysis

In order to examine participants' prediction and derive a measure of predictive ability, we compared their anticipatory looks on the target objects during the critical region (i.e., verb + determiner) between the Biasing (*ride the bike*) and the Neutral conditions (*need the bike*). For this analysis, we first excluded the trials with incorrect mouse-clicking responses. This process resulted in 0.1% data loss.

Then, we calculated the fixation proportions on target and other objects in each condition for each 20ms time bin relative to the onset of the verb using VWPre package (Porretta et al., 2017) in R (R Core Team, 2016). We replaced 0s with 0.01 and 1s with 0.99 (Huettig & Janse, 2016) to calculate the log ratio of fixation proportions on target and other objects. We log transformed the ratios to make the data distribution more suitable (less skewed) for statistical analysis. This log transformed value from 200ms to 842ms after the onset of the verb was used as a dependent variable in a linear mixed effects model to examine participants' prediction. This time window was set considering the saccadic latency – approximately 200ms delay between an external signal and the initiation of a saccadic eye movement (cf. Allopenna, Magnuson, and Tanenhaus, 1998) - and the duration of the critical region (verb +determiner) was 642 ms in the Prediction phase. The model which was constructed using the lme4 package (Bates et al., 2015) included contrast coded Condition (Neutral condition coded as -0.5 and Bias condition coded as 0.5) as a fixed factor, and random intercepts for participants and items and random slopes for Condition by participants, as justified by the research design (Barr, 2008). Reported p-values were calculated using lmerTest package (Kuznetsova, Brockhoff, & Christensen, 2017).

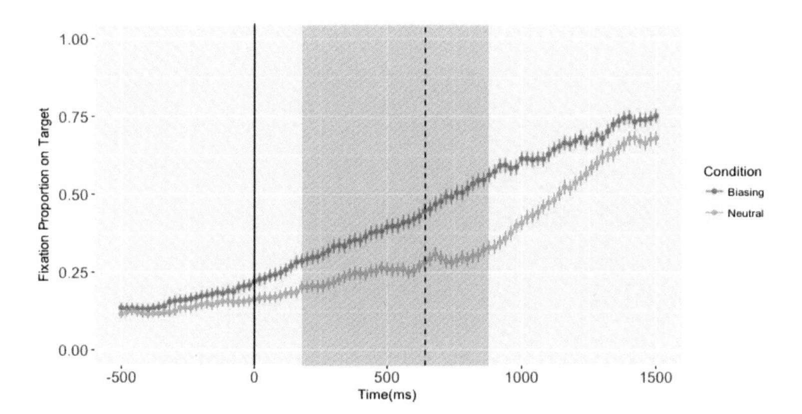

Figure 5-1. Fixation proportions on the target objects (e.g., bike) between the Biasing condition (ride the bike) and Neutral condition (need the bike) in the Prediction phase. Time 0ms: the onset of the verb. The dotted line: the onset of the target noun. The gray region: predictive looks while listening to the verb + the. (error-bars: SE around the mean).

Figure 5-1 plots fixation proportions on target objects in two conditions. The time is synchronized to the verb onset (at 0 ms); the time window of the graph is from -500 ms (i.e., 500 ms before the onset of the verb) to 1500ms, which covers the duration of the critical time (i.e., verb + the: 642ms) corresponding to the gray region in the figure. As shown in Figure 5-1, fixation proportions on target objects became greater in the Biasing condition than in the Neutral condition as soon as participants heard the verbs.

This difference in fixation proportions on the target objects between two conditions was supported by results of the linear mixed effects model. The listeners started to fixate the targets upon hearing the verbs (0~180ms; $b = 0.63$, $SE = 0.23$, $t = 2.71$, $p < .007$) and increasingly fixated the targets more than the competitors during the critical region (the main effect of Condition during 200-842ms: $b = 1.38$, $SE = 0.25$, $t = 5.55$, $p < .0001$). These results indicate that our hypothesis was borne out. Native speakers of English tend to predict upcoming information such as nouns (using semantic properties of verbs) even before hearing these nouns and show anticipatory looks on the items these nouns refer to.

However, participants seemed to differ in terms of their predictive ability as seen in Figure 5-2. This individual predictive ability was calculated by the mean difference in log ratio of fixation proportions on target objects and on other objects between two conditions (i.e., [log(fixation proportions on the target/ fixation proportions on the others) from the Biasing condition] - [log(fixation proportions on the target/ fixation proportions on the others) from the Neutral condition]) during the critical time window for prediction (i.e., 200-842 ms post-verb onset).

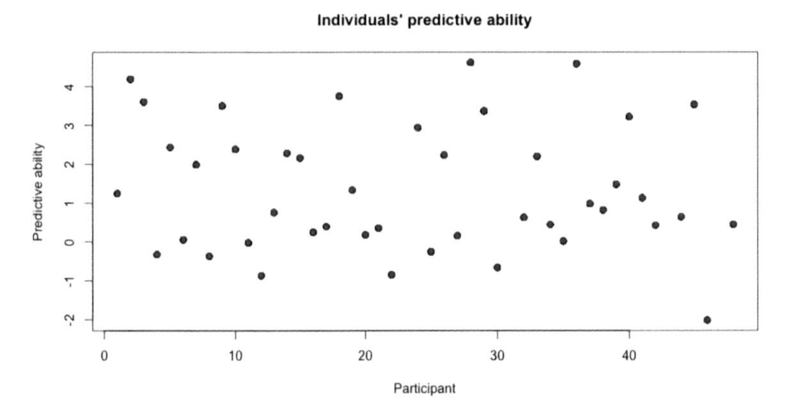

Figure 5-2. Each participant's predictive ability calculated by the mean difference in log ratio of fixation proportions on target objects and on other objects between two conditions (Biasing vs. Neutral)

The mean scores of individuals' predictive ability was 1.34 (SD = 1.56, range: -2.02- 4.61). The log-ratios enable us to measure their prediction and the magnitude of their prediction (Arai, van Gompel & Scheepers, 2007). The score of zero means their looks on the targets compared to those on the others were not different between two conditions. A positive score means more looks to the targets in the Biasing condition than in the Neutral condition (i.e., prediction); and the negative means the opposite. As the measure is symmetrical around zero, its absolute score reflects the magnitude of difference in predictive looks between two conditions (i.e., magnitude of prediction). This measure of predictive ability will be used later as a factor (individuals' predictive ability) in the analysis of the data of the adaptation phase.

Adaptation Phase

♦ ♦ ♦

Offline Adaptation Tasks (Pre- and Post-tests)

This study mainly aimed to investigate whether the interactions between individuals' parsing bias and predictive ability influence adaptation. Under the error- based learning accounts emphasizing the role of prediction, we predicted that 1) participants would show greater adaptation after exposure to their less preferred structures than to their preferred structures, as it is expected that they experience larger prediction error while processing less preferred structures, and 2) this adaptation toward HA would be greater as listeners have greater predictive ability and stronger LA pre- bias (i.e., initial bias).

In order to test these predictions, we used a pre-post design to examine listeners' offline adaptation toward a specific structure after exposure to that structure (i.e., the post-test 1 after exposure to their preferred structure LA, and the post-test 2 after exposure to their less preferred structure, HA). We identified participants' pre-bias (or initial bias) at the pre-test, and aimed to observe change in their bias towards an LA interpretation at the post-tests after each exposure stage. Note that we only included data from participants with LA bias (determined by the pre-test) for analysis due to lack of participants with HA bias. Figure 5-3 illustrates individuals' scores of LA interpretation at the pre-test; the participants showed LA preference with some individual variance.

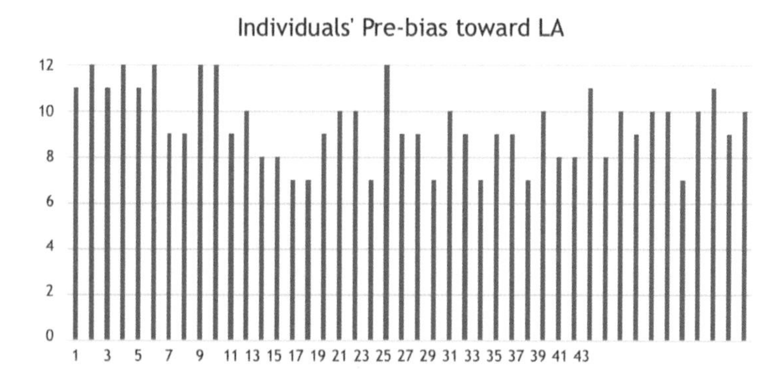

Figure 5-3. Forty-four participants' scores of LA interpretation (out of 12 ambiguous RC attachment sentences) at the pre-test

Figure 5-4 shows how many ambiguous RC sentences out of 12 were interpreted as LA at each test. At the pre-test, participants mostly attached the RC to the NP2 in ambiguous sentences (M=9.43, SD=1.59, range: 7-12). Then, their LA interpretation increased at the post-test 1 (M=10.57, SD=1.84, range: 5-12) after exposure to LA block, but decreased at the post-test 2 (M=8.18, SD=2.95, range: 1-12) after exposure to HA block.

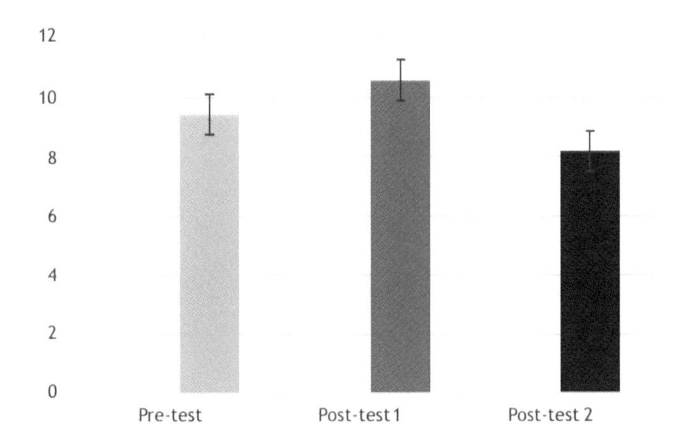

Figure 5-4. Mean number of sentences interpreted as LA (out of 12 ambiguous RC attachment sentences) at the pre- and post-tests (error-bars: SE around the mean)

These results suggest that their interpretation of ambiguous RC sentences was influenced by exposure to each type of attachment, namely adaptation occurred. However, their general preference to LA was not changed; they did not reverse their preference after HA exposure.

To investigate whether this adaptation was guided by the interactions between individuals' predictive ability and parsing bias (i.e., pre-bias), we conducted a logistic linear mixed-effects model on LA interpretations (i.e., the dependent variable: coded as "1" when ambiguous RC sentences were interpreted as LA and coded as "0" when interpreted as HA). For the fixed effects, we included: 1) Predictive ability (measured from the prediction task: the mean difference in log ratio of fixation proportions on target objects and on other objects between two conditions), 2) Pre-bias (LA interpretation scores from the pre-test), 3) Test (Pre-test, Post-test 1 after exposure to the LA block, and Post-test 2 after exposure to the HA block), 4) two-way interactions between Test and each of the other factors, 5) a two-way interaction between Predictive ability and Pre-bias, and 6) a triple interaction between Predictive ability, Pre-bias, and Test.

The fixed factors of Predictive ability and Pre-bias were centered around the mean to help interpretation of coefficients for interaction effects (Baayen, 2008). For the Test, we used dummy coding to see the difference in LA interpretation 1) between Pre-test and Post-test 1 (adaptation toward LA), and 2) between Pre-test and Post-test 2 (adaptation toward HA). This model included random intercepts for participants and items, and by- participant random slopes for Test to resolve non-independences in the data caused by the same participants.

Table 5-2 summarizes results from the logistic mixed-effects model. As can be seen in Table 5-2, those who had stronger LA pre-bias showed more LA interpretations overall (the main effect of Pre-bias: b = 0.59, SE = 0.09, $z = 6.71$, $p < .001$).

Table 5-2. The results from the logistic mixed-effects model on LA interpretations as a function of Predictive ability, Pre-bias and Test

Fixed effects:	b	*SE*	*z*	*p*
(Intercept)	1.62	0.19	8.48	0.00***
Predictive ability	-0.01	0.08	-0.09	0.93
Pre-bias	0.59	0.09	6.71	0.00***
Pre-test vs. Post-test 1	1.29	0.39	3.35	0.00***
Pre-test vs. Post-test 2	-0.51	0.25	-2.05	0.04*
Predictive ability: Pre-bias	-0.00	0.05	-0.06	0.95
Predictive ability: Pre-test vs. Post-test 1	-0.33	0.22	-1.47	0.14
Predictive ability: Pre-test vs. Post-test 2	-0.05	0.15	-0.35	0.72
Pre-bias: Pre-test vs. Post-test 1	-0.11	0.23	-0.47	0.64
Pre-bias: Pre-test vs. Post-test 2	-0.34	0.16	-2.16	0.03*
Predictive ability: Pre-bias: Pre-test vs. Post-test 1	0.03	0.14	0.20	0.84
Predictive ability: Pre-bias: Pre-test vs. Post-test 2	0.06	0.09	0.69	0.49

***p < 0.001, **p < 0.01, *p < 0.05, +p < 0.10
Model: LA Response ~ cPredictive ability * cPre-bias * Test + (1+Test | Participants) + (1|Items)

After exposure to the LA block, participants showed significant adaptation toward LA (the main effect of Pre-test vs. Post-test 1: b = 1.29, SE = 0.39, z = 3.35, p < .001); they were more likely to assign LA interpretations to the ambiguous RCs after the LA exposure block. They also showed significant adaptation toward HA, assigning less LA interpretations after the HA block (the main effect of Pre-test vs. Post-test 2: b = -0.51, SE = 0.25, z = -2.05, p = .04). Importantly, there was a significant interaction effect between Pre-bias and Post-test 2 (b = -0.34, SE = 0.16, z = -2.16, p = .03); participants with stronger LA bias showed greater adaptation toward HA. However, we could not find two-way interactions between Predictive ability and Pre-bias, and between Predictive ability and Test, or a three-way interaction effect between Predictive ability, Test, and Pre-bias. In other words, results of the offline pre-and post-tests did not provide clear evidence as to whether their adaptation was influenced by the interactions between their predictive ability and parsing bias.

Online Adaptation Tasks

Using the visual world paradigm (VWP), we also investigated participants' online adaptation during their exposure to the LA block and the HA block. The exposure stage to each structure is believed to reveal a more dynamic picture about ongoing adaptation, namely, how they adapt to each structure over time, and more crucially, whether their adaptation is influenced by prediction error resulting from interaction between their predictive ability and pre-bias. During each exposure stage, participants were again presented with visual displays and listened to auditory sentences. For the same reason as the Prediction phase, they were required to click the last mentioned items on the presented visual displays. Additionally, we used comprehension questions for online adaptation tasks to see how they interpreted auditory sentences. Since we were interested in prediction change over the course of the experiment, we analyzed eye-tracking data, dividing the trials by quartiles (i.e., 14 trials for each quartile).

Adaptation task 1 (exposure to low attachment, LA)

In the first online adaptation task, participants were exposed to their preferred structure, LA (e.g., I see the cat of the woman that will wear the shoes) accompanied with visual displays containing picture items which can be potential themes of target verbs depending on how to resolve RC attachment. In the case of the given example sentence, two potential themes of the target verb (e.g., wear) were the shoes (that the woman is likely to wear) and the collar (that the cat is likely to wear). Low attachment is more plausible for this example sentence, thus the picture item of shoes was set as a target and the item of the collar was set as a competitor.

Under the error-based learning accounts, it was expected that participants with LA bias would show greater anticipatory looks on the targets (e.g., *the shoes*) compared to the competitors (e.g., *the collar*) as they are assumed to predict based on their parsing bias. As listeners have stronger LA bias and greater predictive ability, they are expected to show more anticipatory looks to the targets at earlier times, and this pattern would be the same to the end of this block because they would rarely experience prediction errors. On the other hand, listeners with weaker LA bias and greater predictive ability may increase their looks on the targets over time as they repeatedly encounter LA sentences in this block (i.e., effects of recent experience with LA sentences on adaptation).

Behavioral tasks accuracy

Participants showed high accuracy in mouse- clicking responses (M = 55.79 out of 56 trials, SD = 0.46) and in comprehension questions in the LA block (M = 35 out of 37 trials (90%), SD = 2.29). These results indicate that participants paid attention to the task, and interpreted most sentences as LA.

Eye-tracking data analysis

From eye-tracking data in the online adaptation task, we expected to find that participants' anticipatory looks change over the course of the experiment as a result of adaptation. As was the case in the analysis for eye-tracking data in the Prediction phase, we first excluded the trials with incorrect mouse- clicking responses (0.4% data loss) and then the trials with the incorrect comprehension answers. This exclusion was to make it sure that for analysis we used the data collected when participants were attentively listening to the sentences and made correct LA interpretations. This elimination process resulted in 3.3% data loss in total. Then, we calculated the fixation proportions on the targets and on the competitors in each condition for each 20ms time bin relative to the onset of the verb using the VWPre package.

Figure 5-5 plots averaged fixation proportions on the targets (e.g., *shoes*) and the competitors (e.g., *collar*) from all the trials in the LA block. As can be seen in Figure 5-5, participants with LA bias showed slightly more anticipatory looks to the targets than the competitors while listening to sentences aligning with their parsing bias (LA).

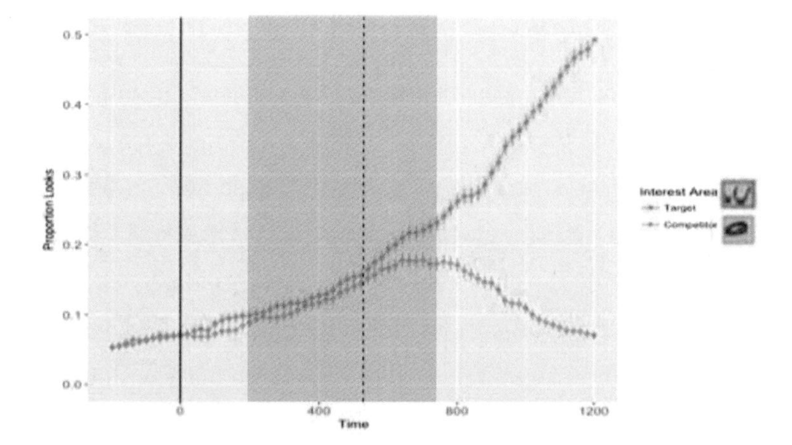

Figure 5-5. Averaged fixation proportions on the targets and competitors in the LA block. Time 0ms: the onset of the verb. The dotted line: the onset of the target noun. The gray region: predictive looks while listening to the verb + the.(error-bars: SE around the mean).

According to results of a one sample t-test, the difference in looks between the targets and the competitors was significantly greater than zero ($t(43091) = 7.36$, $p < .0001$), suggesting that participants looked more at the targets than the competitors during the target region (*verb* + *the*) in the LA block.

As we were interested in participants' anticipatory looks over time, we compared fixation proportions on the targets with those on the competitors during the critical period (i.e., 200~726ms post-verb onset) by breaking down trials by quartiles (i.e., 14 trials for each quartile). Figure 5-6 illustrates averaged fixation proportions on the targets (e.g., *shoes*) and the competitors (e.g., *collar*) over the quartiles. As in Figure 5-6, participants showed slightly more anticipatory looks to the competitors (i.e., predictive looks to incorrect items) at first but these looks decreased over time after repeated exposure to LA sentences (e.g., *I see the cat of the woman that will wear the shoes*).

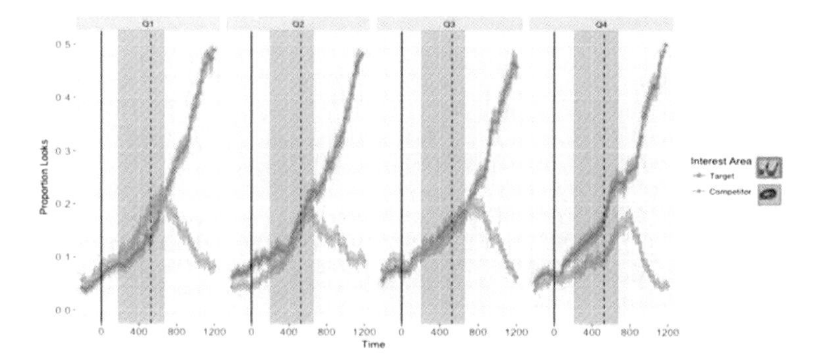

Figure 5-6. LA block: fixation proportions on the targets and competitors over time (4 quartiles). Time 0ms: the onset of the verb. The dotted line: the onset of the target noun. The gray region: predictive looks while listening to the verb + the. (error-bars: SE around the mean). Q1 refers to the first quartile (i.e., the first 14 trials) and Q4 refers to the last quartile (i.e., the last 14 trials).

Once comparing the data at Q1 (i.e., trials at the beginning) with the data at Q4 (i.e., trials at the end of the experiment), we can clearly see how their prediction changed; their looks to the competitors decreased, instead their looks to the targets increased such that anticipatory looks to the targets became greater than those to the competitors at the end (Q4).

For the analysis to see whether change of their looks over time, as revealed in Figure 5-6, is statistically significant, we constructed a linear mixed effects model. For the dependent variable, we used target advantage scores by calculating the difference in fixation proportions between target and competitor objects ([proportions on the targets] – [proportions on the competitors]) during the critical time window (i.e., 200~726 ms post-verb onset). This critical period – which is expected to show participants' predictive processing - was set as eye movements reflecting language processing are reported to be observed approximately from 200 ms after listening to stimuli, and the duration for the target region (*verb +determiner*) is 526 ms.

For the fixed factors, we included Predictive ability (measured from the prediction task: the mean difference in log ratio of fixation proportions on target objects and on other objects between two conditions), Pre-bias (LA interpretation scores from the pre-test), Quartiles (Q1~4), and all possible two-way and three-way interactions between the fixed factors mentioned above. Predictive ability and Pre-bias were centered to help interpretation of coefficients for interaction effects (Baayen, 2008). The factor of Quartiles (Q1~4) was dummy coded (Q1 coded as reference level) as we compared 'target advantage scores' of each quartile with those of the first quartile (Q1).

For random effects, we included random intercepts for participants and items, and by-participant random slopes for Quartiles, as justified by the research design. If the change of participants' prediction over time was influenced by their predictive ability and pre-bias, we expected to find interaction effects between Pre-bias, Predictive ability, and Quartiles.

As shown in Table 5-3 which summarizes results of this mixed effects model, there was a significant effect of Quartile 4 ($b = 0.09$, $SE = 0.04$, $t = 2.26$, $p = .03$); the difference in looks between the targets and the competitors at Q4 was significantly different from Q1. Participants showed significantly greater anticipatory looks to the competitors ($t(10421) = -4.36$, $p < .0001$) at the beginning of the LA block (Q1), but their looks to the targets increased, resulting in significantly more looks to the targets than the competitors at Q4. However, there were no significant two-way or three-way interactions.

Table 5-3. LA block: the results of the mixed effects model on target advantage scores as a function of Predictive ability, Pre-bias and Quartiles in the adaptation task 1.

Fixed effects:	*b*	*SE*	*t*	*p*
(Intercept)	-0.03	0.03	-0.95	0.34
Predictive ability	0.01	0.01	0.57	0.57
Pre-bias	-0.00	0.01	-0.04	0.96
Quartile 2	0.06	0.04	1.44	0.15
Quartile 3	0.04	0.04	0.89	0.38
Quartile 4	0.09	0.04	2.26	0.03*
Predictive ability: Pre-bias	0.00	0.01	0.09	0.93
Predictive ability: Quartile 2	-0.00	0.02	-0.02	0.99
Predictive ability: Quartile 3	0.01	0.02	0.52	0.60
Predictive ability: Quartile 4	-0.01	0.02	-0.36	0.72
Pre-bias: Quartile 2	-0.01	0.02	-0.75	0.45
Pre-bias: Quartile 3	0.00	0.02	0.24	0.81
Pre-bias: Quartile 4	0.00	0.02	0.18	0.86
Predictive ability: Pre-bias: Quartile 2	0.01	0.01	1.11	0.27
Predictive ability: Pre-bias: Quartile 3	-0.00	0.01	-0.36	0.72
Predictive ability: Pre-bias: Quartile 4	-0.00	0.01	-0.17	0.86

***p < 0.001, **p < 0.01, *p < 0.05, +p < 0.10

Model: Target advantage score ~ cPredictive ability * cPre-bias * Quartiles + (1+Quartiles| Participants) + (1| Items)

Adaptation task 2 (exposure to high attachment, HA)

In the second online adaptation task, the participants were exposed to their less preferred structure, HA (e.g., I see the cat of the woman that will wear the collar). Under the error-based learning accounts, we expected that participants with LA bias would show greater anticipatory looks on the competitors (e.g., shoes) at the beginning of their exposure to HA, as they predict based on parsing bias LA. However, this pattern of prediction would lead them to experience prediction errors, which results in adaptation that would influence their future predictions. Therefore, their prediction as a result of adaptation would be changed over time such that they would show more anticipatory looks on the targets (e.g., collar) at the end. This change was expected to be greater for those who had stronger LA bias and greater predictive ability, presumably experiencing larger prediction errors.

Behavioral task accuracy

Participants showed high accuracy rate in mouse- clicking responses (M = 55.72 out of 56 trials, SD=0.45) indicating that participants paid attention to the task. The mean accuracy for the comprehension questions in the HA block was 31.68 out of 39 trials (82%, SD=4.37), relatively lower than their accuracy in the LA block.

Eye-tracking data analysis

We omitted data from 2 participants with low accuracy (e.g., scores less than the value of (Mean - 2.5 SD) for the comprehension questions). Then, we used exactly the same procedure with the data analysis for the Adaptation task 1 (exposure to the LA sentences). Excluding the trials with incorrect mouse-clicking responses in the HA block yielded 0.4% data loss, and then eliminating those with incorrect comprehension answers resulted in 12 % data loss in total.

Figure 5-7 plots averaged fixation proportions on the targets (e.g., *collar*) and the competitors (e.g., *shoes*) in the HA block, revealing overall prediction while participants were listening to their less preferred structures. In contrast to the LA block, the listeners' looks to the competitors seemed slightly greater until they heard the target nouns; but results of a one sample t-test revealed no significant difference in looks between the targets and the competitors ($t(38069) = -1.85, p = .06$).

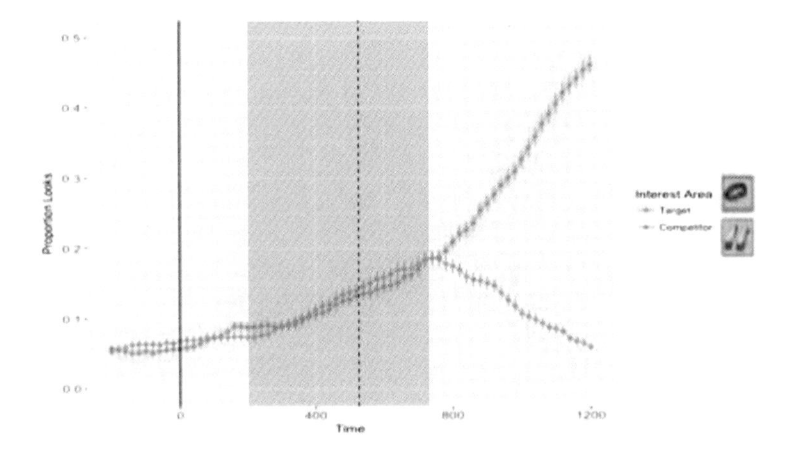

Figure 5-7. Averaged fixation proportions on the targets and competitors in the HA block. Time 0ms: the onset of the verb. The vertical dotted line: the onset of the target noun. The gray region: predictive looks while listening to the verb + the.

Figure 5-8 illustrates averaged fixation proportions on the targets (e.g., *collar*) and the competitors (e.g., *shoes*) over the quartiles. As seen in Figure 5-8, participants showed more anticipatory looks to the competitors at first – for a longer time (Q1 & Q2) than in the LA block; the difference in looks between the targets and the competitors at the HA block was significant at Q1 ($t(8882) = -1.97$, $p = .05$) and at Q2 ($t(9827) = -5.50$, $p < .0001$). However, these predictive looks to incorrect items decreased over time, and their looks to the targets gradually increased but not to the extent of showing greater looks to the targets until the end.

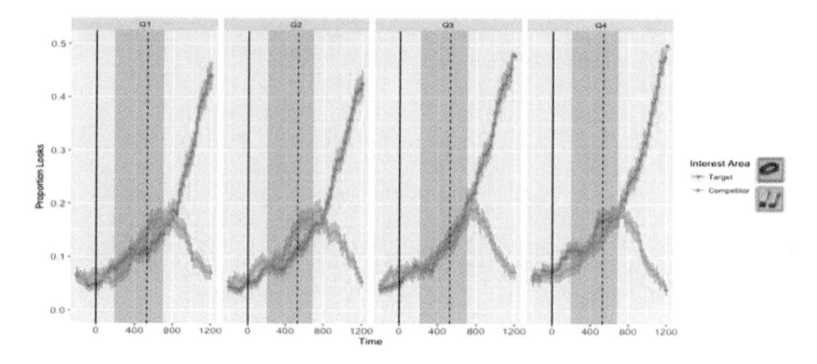

Figure 5-8. HA block: fixation proportions on the targets and competitors over time (4 quartiles). Time 0ms: the onset of the verb. The vertical dotted line: the onset of the target noun. The gray region: predictive looks while listening to the verb + the.

Again, for the statistical analysis to investigate whether change of participants' predictive looks over time (i.e., prediction change as a result of adaptation) was influenced by their predictive ability and pre-bias, we constructed a linear mixed effects model in the same way we did for the eye-tracking data analysis in the adaptation task1. Table 5-4 provides the summary of results from this mixed effects model.

As shown in Table 5-4, there were no significant main effects. Listeners with LA bias, as expected, showed more predictive looks to incorrect items (i.e., the competitors) at the beginning, and these prediction errors decreased as they repeatedly encountered HA sentences. However, this pattern of change in their predictive looks was not statistically significant. Importantly, there was a significant interaction between Pre-bias and Quartile 3 ($b = 0.05$, $SE = 0.02$, $t = 2.19$, $p = .03$); the stronger bias toward LA, the greater looks to the targets at Q3 relative to at Q1.

Table 5-4. HA block: the results of the mixed effects model on target advantage scores as a function of Predictive ability, Pre-bias and Quartiles in the adaptation task 2

Fixed effects:	*b*	*SE*	*t*	*p*
(Intercept)	-0.01	0.03	-0.49	0.62
Predictive ability	-0.01	0.01	-0.40	0.69
Pre-bias	-0.01	0.01	-0.63	0.53
Quartile 2	-0.01	0.04	-0.37	0.71
Quartile 3	0.03	0.04	0.64	0.53
Quartile 4	0.02	0.04	0.63	0.53
Predictive ability : Pre-bias	-0.00	0.01	-0.46	0.65
Predictive ability : Quartile 2	0.01	0.02	0.84	0.41
Predictive ability : Quartile 3	-0.01	0.02	-0.27	0.79
Predictive ability : Quartile 4	0.03	0.02	1.41	0.17
Pre-bias: Quartile 2	-0.01	0.02	-0.41	0.68
Pre-bias: Quartile 3	0.05	0.02	2.19	0.03*
Pre-bias: Quartile 4	0.01	0.02	0.28	0.78
Predictive ability : Pre-bias: Quartile 2	-0.00	0.01	-0.23	0.82
Predictive ability : Pre-bias: Quartile 3	-0.00	0.01	-0.25	0.80
Predictive ability : Pre-bias: Quartile 4	0.00	0.01	0.30	0.77

***p < 0.001, **p < 0.01, *p < 0.05, +p < 0.10

Model: Target advantage score ~ cPredictive ability * cPre-bias * Quartiles + (1+Quartiles | Participants) + (1| Items)

To further examine this interaction effect, we divided participants into two groups using their pre-bias: stronger vs. weaker bias group. The stronger bias group included participants who scored equal to or greater than 10 LA interpretations at the pre-test and the weaker bias group included participants who scored greater than 6 and less than 10 LA interpretations. Figure 5-9 and Figure 5-10 plot changes in fixation proportions on the targets and the competitors over the quartiles in the stronger bias group and in the weaker bias group, respectively. As seen in these plots, relative to at Q1, those with stronger LA bias showed significantly greater looks to the targets than to the competitors at Q3 whereas those with weaker LA bias kept showing more looks to the competitors.

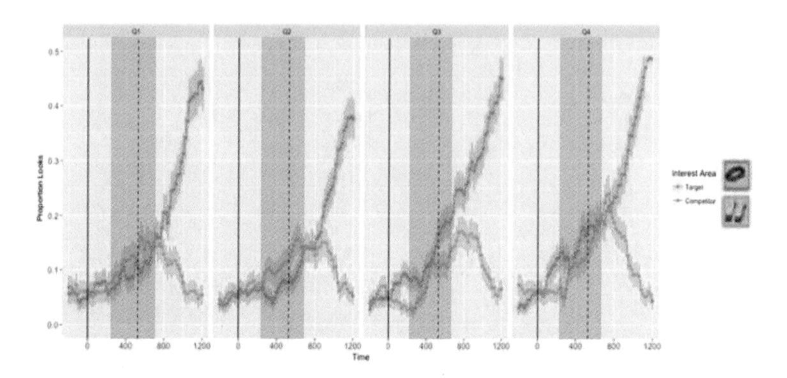

Figure 5-9. HA block: fixation proportions on the targets and competitors over the quartiles in the stronger bias group.

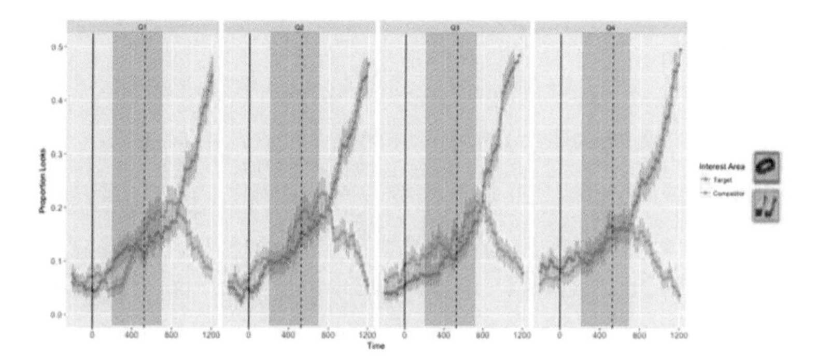

Figure 5-10. HA block: fixation proportions on the targets and competitors over the quartiles in the weaker bias group.

Summary of Findings

♦ ♦ ♦

At the offline pre-and post-tests, native speakers of English with LA bias showed significant adaptation toward their preferred structure, LA as well as less preferred structure, HA. The significant interaction between pre-bias and adaptation toward HA suggested that the stronger LA bias listeners had, the greater adaptation toward HA they showed. However, we did not find any effects of predictive ability on adaptation, or interaction effects between predictive ability and pre-bias on adaptation at the offline pre- and post-tests. According to the results from online adaptation tasks, while listening to LA sentences (preferred structure) in the first adaptation task, participants showed slightly more looks to the competitors at first (Q1) but these incorrect predictions (prediction errors) decreased over time, ultimately showing significant difference in looks at the end (Q4) - more looks to the targets than to the competitors - relative to at the beginning (Q1).

However, this prediction change during exposure to LA sentences was not influenced by different degrees of pre-bias or predictive ability. In the second online adaptation task in which participants were exposed to HA sentences (input against their bias), participants showed numerically more anticipatory looks to the competitors (prediction errors) at the beginning for a longer period of time (up to Q2). This pattern of incorrect predictions decreased over time again but not to the extent of showing greater looks to the targets until the end of the HA block. Importantly, however, the significant interaction effect between pre-bias and quartile 3 suggested that the listeners with stronger LA bias showed greater looks to the targets than to the competitors at Q3 relative to at Q1. These results are discussed in more detail in Chapter 6.

DISCUSSION & CONCLUSION

UNLOCKING THE POWER OF ADAPTATION

CHAPTER

06

In this study, we investigated the role of prediction in adaptation by testing the hypothesis generated from the core assertions of the error-based learning accounts. The error-based learning accounts posit a crucial role of prediction in adaptation, claiming that language users make predictions based on their previous linguistic experience (e.g., bias) and adapt to the current linguistic input in case of experiencing prediction errors (i.e., mismatch between their predictions and actual linguistic input).

These assertions suggest that the extent of adaptation may be determined by listeners' sensitivity to prediction errors, and this sensitivity supposedly comes from interactions between their predictive ability and parsing bias. The stronger bias and greater predictive ability listeners have, the larger prediction errors they can experience, which would lead to greater adaptation. Therefore, we specifically hypothesized that an individual's adaptation is guided by prediction error, presumably resulting from interactions between their parsing bias and predictive ability.

To test this hypothesis, in this study we operationalized prediction as anticipatory looks to target items before hearing target words in the visual world paradigms. We measured the degree of each listener's parsing bias using relative clause (RC) attachment bias. Similar to verb bias, RC attachment bias is known as being shaped by life-long experience. This aspect made it suitable for the current experiment as it allowed us to observe whether listeners make predictions based on their parsing bias and experience prediction errors when processing structures against their bias.

In the main experiment consisting of the prediction and the adaptation phases, we measured individuals' predictive ability (using the prediction task) and initial parsing bias regarding RC attachment (using the offline pre-test). After that, we observed whether predictive ability and bias thus defined influenced their adaptation during exposure to their preferred structure, LA (in the online adaptation 1 task) and during exposure to their less preferred structure, HA (in the online adaptation 2 task), and finally adaptation after the exposure to each type of attachment (at the post-tests). As we made three predictions to test the hypothesis that individuals' adaptation is guided by prediction error resulting from interactions between bias and predictive ability, I will discuss the findings regarding these predictions below.

Adaptation at the Offline Pre-and Post-tests

♦ ♦ ♦

Prediction 1

In the off-line pre- and post-tests, it was predicted that listeners with LA bias would show greater adaptation toward their less preferred structure, HA sentences, as they would experience more prediction errors while processing HA sentences. This pattern would be stronger for listeners with stronger LA bias and greater predictive ability (i.e., interaction effect between predictive ability and bias), because they are expected to experience larger prediction errors.

In order to test prediction 1, we first identified participants' attachment bias using ambiguous RC attachment sentences in the pre-test. Corresponding to reported preferences for native English speakers (Frazier & Clifton, 1996), most native speakers of English in this study were biased toward low attachment but to various degrees (6~12 LA interpretation out of 12 ambiguous RC sentences), which enabled us to examine the effect of different degrees of bias on prediction and adaptation. In the prediction phase administered immediately after the pre-test, we measured individual participants' predictive ability using their anticipatory looks onto target items of visual displays while they were listening to auditory sentences. According to the results, overall participants showed greater anticipatory looks onto the targets (e.g., *bike*) before hearing the target words when they listened to sentences with RC attachment (e.g., *I meet the father of the boy that will…..*) from the Biasing condition (e.g., *ride the bike*) than from the Neutral condition (e.g., *need the bike*).

In other words, the averaged results across the participants revealed that native speakers of English have a tendency to predict while processing even complex constructions such as RC attachment. This finding is consistent with previous results that native speakers of English tend to predict upcoming information - as evidenced by their anticipatory looks on target items even before hearing the target words in visual-world eye tracking studies - using cues from the context such as semantic property of verbs (Altmann & Kamide, 1999; Kamide, 2012).

This replication of prediction effect indicates that the methodology to measure individuals' predictive ability in this study was valid. Importantly, however, a general tendency to predict does not necessarily mean that every listener is a predictor, or that prediction is used for adaptation. Therefore, for further investigation on the role of prediction in adaptation, we measured individuals' predictive ability, calculated by the mean difference in log ratio of fixation proportions on target objects and on other objects between two conditions (Biasing vs. Neutral). Surprisingly, individual listeners greatly differed in terms of predictive ability even though they were all native speakers of English (Figure 5-2). This finding lends support to the necessity of the current study exploring the effects of individuals' different degrees of predictive ability on adaptation to have a better picture about the role of prediction in adaptation.

Statistical models analyzing the data from the pre- and post-tests using individual's predictive ability and LA attachment bias revealed that there was significant change in LA interpretation after exposure to each structure type, suggesting that adaptation occurred not only toward LA but toward HA as well. Participants' LA interpretations significantly increased after exposure to the LA block and decreased after exposure to the HA block. This finding is compatible with the results from priming studies in comprehension including Pickering et al. (2013) and Kim et al. (2014). In a priming study using a sentence-picture matching task, Pickering et al. (2013) found that native English speakers tend to interpret globally ambiguous sentences (e.g. *The waitress prodding the clown with the umbrella*) as high-attachment after comprehending a high-attachment prime sentence (e.g. when a sentence *The policeman prodding the doctor with the gun* was matched to a picture that described the policeman using the gun to prod the doctor). This priming effect occurred independently of lexical overlap, and persisted across intervening sentences (i.e., long-lasting effect).

Similarly, Kim et al (2014) reported that native English speakers were more likely to interpret globally ambiguous sentences (e.g., *The FBI agent noticed the mirror on the wall with the crack*) as low attachment after reading low-attachment sentences (e.g., *The party took place at the house in the alley with the potholes*). They also read a target sentence faster when they parsed the target sentence using the prime structure (i.e., facilitated reading as a result of priming). Though we did not use a priming paradigm in this study, participants showed influence of exposure to each type of attachment in a block design. After exposure to the LA block where only LA sentences were presented (with filler sentences), participants were more likely to interpret ambiguous RC sentences as LA whereas they were less likely to interpret ambiguous RC sentences as LA (i.e., adaptation toward HA) after exposure to the HA block where only HA sentences were presented (with filler sentences).

Significant adaptation toward a preferred structure (e.g., low attachment interpretation) may seem surprising, but it is possible given that participants in this study had different degrees of LA bias; those with weaker LA bias may have had much room for adaptation toward LA. Adaptation toward preferred structures was also reported from priming studies (e.g., Kaschak, 2007; Kaschak, Kutta, & Schatschneider, 2011) in which experimental settings were compatible with those in the current study. After exposure to 100% DO biasing condition in which they were forced to complete sentence stems as a DO construction, native speakers of English – known to be biased toward a DO construction– were more likely to complete target stems (that can be finished either a DO or a PO construction) as a DO construction than those who were exposed to 100% PO biasing condition. The same pattern of target completion was observed even 7 days after exposure to 100% DO biasing condition (Kaschak et al., 2011), suggesting that this kind of cumulative adaptation is long-lasting.

In addition, as expected, those with stronger LA bias showed greater adaptation toward HA. This finding is in keeping with previous results, namely, the inverse frequency/preference effect (e.g., Farmer et al., 2011; Kim et al., 2014). Native English speakers in Farmer et al. (2011)'s study showed longer reading times at the main verb (disambiguating region, e.g., "*conducted*") while reading reduced relative clauses (RC, e.g., *The experienced soldiers warned about the dangers conducted the midnight raid"*) because they were more biased toward main clause continuations and initially interpreted "*warned*" as the main verb of the sentence. Over time, they adapted to reduced relative clauses and showed reduced reading times at the disambiguating region. Their adaptation for less frequent structures (reduced relative clauses) was greater than for more frequent structures (main clause continuations), evidenced by faster reading times for the disambiguating region in the reduced relative clauses than for the counterpart in main clause continuations. This inverse frequency/preference effect was predicted under the error-based learning accounts; greater adaptation toward less preferred structures can be explained due to larger prediction errors while processing them. More weight changes to reduce future prediction errors would result in greater adaptation toward less preferred structures.

However, the findings from the offline pre-and post-tests can also be accounted for using belief-updating models which posit that language users rapidly update their syntactic beliefs in the current context considering statistics of structures and reliability of cues regarding structures. In our study, participants may incrementally update their syntactic expectations or beliefs to make their processing more efficient. For example, when they were increasingly exposed to LA sentences in the LA block, they could rapidly update their syntactic expectations about LA (i.e., a probability distribution over LA structure) using their recent linguistic experience (i.e., repeated exposure to LA) and reliable cues (e.g., semantic constraints that were consistently used to manipulate RC attachment).

It should be noted that adaptation toward HA sentences occurred, but not to the extent of changing their bias direction. Participants still assigned more LA interpretations when processing ambiguous RC sentences even after their exposure to the HA block (M=8.06 out of 12). Given that this attachment bias was established throughout their life-time experience with RC sentences, short exposure to the less- preferred construction (56 trials) during the experiment may not have been enough for them to change their bias direction. The main effect of pre-bias on LA interpretations at the post-tests supports this view as those with stronger LA bias showed more LA interpretations overall.

The results from the offline pre-and post-tests did not reveal any effect of individuals' predictive ability or interaction effects with predictive ability on adaptation. Since no studies to date have explored the effect of predictive ability on adaptation yet, this finding cannot yet be directly compared with other studies. The offline pre-and post- tests used only a small number of items (12 trials), which may make it hard to observe any change affected by interactions between predictive ability and pre-bias. This offline methodology also prevented us from observing whether syntactic expectations could be manifested as a form of prediction and updated during online integration of representations. Therefore, we included online adaptation tasks in the main study which were expected to provide a better picture about the role of prediction in adaptation, that is, whether listeners adapt over time making use of prediction errors as claimed in the error-based learning accounts.

Online Adaptation during Exposure to the LA

♦ ♦ ♦

Prediction 2

In the LA block during exposure to their preferred structure, listeners would show more anticipatory looks onto the targets aligning with their LA attachment bias as they are assumed to make predictions based on their bias. For example, those with LA bias would show more anticipatory looks onto *the shoes* than *the collar* as they process sentences with LA (e.g., *I see the cat of the woman that will wear the shoes).* We expected that listeners with stronger LA bias and greater predictive ability would show more anticipatory looks to the targets at earlier times, and this pattern would be the same over time as they rarely experience prediction errors in the LA block. On the other hand, listeners with weaker LA bias and greater predictive ability may increase their looks on the targets as they repeatedly encounter LA sentences in this block (i.e., effect of recent experience with LA sentences).

The first adaptation task was designed to investigate participants' online adaptation during exposure to their preferred structure (LA). Examining change of their anticipatory looks over the quartiles revealed that listeners with LA bias showed slightly more anticipatory looks to the competitors at first (Q1). This pattern can be due to participants having different degrees of LA bias. Those with weaker LA bias may not predict correct items at the beginning of the LA block since their bias was not strong enough to serve as a base for making predictions. Examining eye-tracking data by dividing it into two bias groups (stronger vs. weaker bias) revealed that it was the case; the predictive looks to the competitors at Q1 were mainly from the weaker bias group.

Participants' predictive looks to the competitors (i.e., incorrect predictions), however, decreased over time, and ultimately their looks to the targets were greater than those to the competitors at the end (Q4). Remarkably, their predictive looks at Q4 were significantly different from those at Q1, suggesting that participants made correct predictions at the end aligning with the current linguistic input (LA sentences) as a function of increased exposure to LA structure. This change of participants' predictive looks is considered to reflect online adaptation during exposure to LA sentences.

Participants could make more anticipatory looks to the targets (i.e., correct predictions) at the end, as they adapted their syntactic representations toward LA and used henceforth the updated representations to make predictions. A crucial finding in the LA block is that listeners with LA bias showed significant adaptation after experiencing small prediction errors (predictive looks to the incorrect items) at Q1. It is noteworthy to mention that correct predictions did not appear immediately after these prediction errors, rather it was observed some time later (e.g., after two quartiles). The time between Q1 and Q4 may reflect required time for adjusting weights in linguistic representations and/or memory consolidation.

Online Adaptation during Exposure to the HA

♦ ♦ ♦

Prediction 3

In the HA block during exposure to the less preferred structure, it was expected that listeners with LA bias would show more anticipatory looks to the competitors (incorrect predictions) than to the targets at the beginning of the experiment as they would predict based on their LA bias. As these prediction errors are claimed to lead to adaptation, LA bias participants were expected to change their prediction pattern such that they would show greater anticipatory looks on the targets than the competitors as a result of adaptation toward HA parsing. This pattern would be clearer for those who had stronger LA bias and greater predictive ability (i.e., interaction effects between pre- bias and predictive ability) because they would experience larger prediction errors. The second adaptation task was considered an essential part of this study as this task would provide evidence for the error-based learning accounts, that is, whether listeners experience prediction errors due to prediction based on their bias, use prediction errors for adaptation and consequently change their later predictions.

During exposure to their less preferred structure, HA (e.g., *I see the cat of the woman that will wear the collar*), listeners with LA bias showed more anticipatory looks to the competitors (e.g., shoes) than the targets (e.g., collar) at the beginning of the task (at Q1), as shown in Figure 5-8. This pattern was expected under the error-based learning accounts. Interestingly, their experience of prediction error was longer at the HA block than at the LA block.

Significantly more predictive looks to the competitors were observed only in Q1 at the LA block whereas this pattern lasted up to Q2 at the HA block. This may be due to the listeners' recent adaptation toward LA sentences in the previous block, in addition to their LA bias shaped by their long-term linguistic experience. As this study used similar contexts for online adaptation task 1 (LA block) and 2 (HA block), the adaptation that occurred during the LA block could be easily transferred to the HA block and thus trigger more interference and prediction error. The interference effect in the HA block was also manifested in relatively low accuracy (82%) at comprehension questions by contrast to high accuracy (94%) in the LA block.

As more HA sentences were encountered, however, anticipatory looks to the competitors decreased, similarly to what was observed in the LA block. These anticipatory eye-movement patterns are in agreement with the prediction that we made based on the error-based learning accounts. Since listeners make predictions on the basis of their bias, they would look at more competitors than targets while listening to HA sentences at the beginning of the HA block. After experiencing these prediction errors, participants were further expected to change their prediction in a way that they show more anticipatory looks to the targets (correct predictions) as they adapt toward HA sentences.

The final stage of showing greater predictive looks to the targets was not observed in our data from the HA block. We only observed numerically reduced predictive looks to the competitors and increasing predictive looks to the targets until the end of the block. This may be due to a lack of statistical power because we lost a great deal of data from the HA block for the analysis; compared to the LA block, approximately 4 times as many data points were excluded from statistical analysis due to incorrect comprehension trials.

As discussed above, given that a certain amount of time is required for weight changes in the current syntactic representations and memory consolidation, we may expect to observe increases in looks to the targets (correct predictions) after Q4. Note that correct predictions as a result of adaptation toward LA were observed approximately 2 quartiles after prediction errors. In order to test this possibility, future studies with enhanced statistical power are recommended. They need to increase the number of participants and/or the number of trials such that prediction change can be observed over longer stretch of time.

Even though we could not observe a significant difference in their predictive looks at the end compared to those at the beginning, we found the significant interaction between pre-bias and Q3. This suggests that those with stronger LA bias showed more looks to the targets (i.e., correct predictions) at Q3 compared to Q1 whereas those with weaker LA bias did not significantly increase their looks to the targets. In other words, those with stronger LA bias showed online adaptation at Q3. It is likely that they updated their syntactic expectations in the HA block after experiencing incorrect predictive looks (prediction errors) and changed their predictions toward the current linguistic input, HA.

The significant online adaptation at Q3 interacting with pre-bias supports the inverse frequency effect, compatible with the offline data. An interesting point is that the online adaptation effect did not last to Q4. It may be due to time required for memory consolidation, as mentioned earlier. After prediction errors, consequences of significant adaptation were observed at Q3 particularly in those with stronger bias. They could make correct predictions (i.e., more looks to the targets than to the competitors) as they updated their syntactic expectations about HA sentences in the block in which they were forced to process constructions against their bias. Their updated syntactic representations may need to be reconsolidated, not yielding a robust effect at Q4.

It is also plausible that this pattern reflects a non-linear fashion of change in weights by prediction error in error-based learning mechanisms. As the error–based model employs back propagation to adjust the weights of a simple recurrent network, the process of change in weights using prediction error is expected to result in a highly non- linear relation between prediction error and the strength of adaptation (Jaeger & Snider, 2013).

In summary, the findings of this study suggest that native speakers of English make explicit predictions (pre-activation of upcoming linguistic information) based on cues from the given context, evidenced by their anticipatory eye movements to targets even before hearing the target items. From the adaptation phase, we did not find direct evidence that adaptation is guided by the interactions between individuals' pre-bias and predictive ability; only pre-bias had an effect. We observed that listeners showed incorrect predictive looks (prediction errors) at the beginning of each attachment block; prediction errors lasted for a longer time during exposure to HA, their less preferred structure. Crucially, listeners' looks to the incorrect items (competitors) decreased over time and their predictive looks were changed aligning with the input in each block.

Listeners' predictive looks were significantly different at Q4 (showing greater looks to the targets) compared to at Q1 in the LA block, and those with stronger bias, similarly to the LA block, showed significant change in their predictive looks at Q3 compared to at Q1 in the HA block. After showing changes in their predictions this way, listeners' RC interpretations at the post-tests significantly differed; they increased LA interpretations after exposure to the LA block and decreased LA interpretations after exposure to the HA block. In particular, those with stronger LA bias showed a greater change in predictive looks to the targets between Q1 and Q3 in the HA eyetracking task, and they also showed greater adaptation to HA at (pre- vs.) the posttest2.

These results may imply that there is a close relation between prediction (error) and adaptation. After experiencing some degrees of prediction errors, listeners changed their predictions in a way that they reduced prediction errors and finally showed correct predictions aligning with the current linguistic input (e.g., each type of attachment). In line with the claim that prediction is a by-product of adaptation (Chang et al., 2012), changes in predictions, particularly changes reducing prediction errors, may reflect adjusting weights in syntactic representations (i.e., process of adaptation), which in turn result in correct predictions and change in the interpretations of ambiguous RC sentences. After a certain amount of reduction in prediction errors during Q2 and Q3, correct predictions (adaptation effect) therefore could be observed at the end of the LA block since listeners used the newly updated syntactic representations for prediction.

This adaptation effect was observed in post-test 1 as well; LA interpretations significantly increased after exposure to LA sentences. Recall that there was a discrepancy between online data and offline data in the HA block. Even though we could not observe significantly greater looks to the targets until the end of the HA block, the participants showed significant adaptation toward HA at the post-test 2 after exposure to this block. This may then be because adaptation could occur during Q3 and Q4 when prediction errors were gradually reduced via changes in weights. In other words, the stage of reduction in prediction errors may help us estimate whether there would be adaptation or not. Correct predictions at the end may just enable us to reaffirm the effect of adaptation. Likewise, the stage of reduction in prediction errors is considered crucial for adaptation and this stage was found from the eye-tracking data during exposure to the HA block. Therefore, it seems possible that we found listeners' significant adaptation toward HA at the post-test 2 after exposure to HA sentences, even though we could not observe adaptation effects (i.e., significantly greater anticipatory looks to targets than competitors) across the board in the eye-tracking data.

Theoretical Implications

♦ ♦ ♦

With the aim of investigating the role of prediction in adaptation, this study observed adult native English speakers' syntactic adaptation during and after exposure to different types of RC attachment. Adaptation observed after exposure to each attachment type (i.e., the results from offline pre-and post-tests) can be explained by accounts employing implicit learning mechanism such as the ACT-R model, the error- based learning accounts and the belief-updating account. First, according to the ACT-R model, the base-level activation of each attachment type could be increased every time listeners encountered a specific attachment, resulting in adaptation after the exposure stage. Alternatively, the adaptation at the pre-and post-tests can be explained by using the notion of prediction error proposed in the error-based learning accounts.

Participants may experience different degrees of prediction errors during the exposure to each type of attachment. Then, the summed prediction errors may lead them to adapt to each attachment type after the exposure stage. Different degrees of prediction errors can explain the inverse frequency effect – the greater adaptation toward HA in those with stronger LA bias. Finally, we can also explain this adaptation using the belief updating account. We manipulated RC attachment using semantic constraint such as world knowledge, thus the semantic constraint could serve as a reliable cue. Moreover, only one type of attachment was used in each block, so statistical properties of a specific RC interpretation could be easily tracked by listeners. Therefore, as proposed in the belief updating account, listeners in this study may update their syntactic expectations considering the consistent semantic cue and statistical distributions of a specific attachment in each block with increasing exposure to the attachment.

Ultimately, updating their syntactic beliefs could yield significant adaptation. Again, depending on their parsing bias, the extent of update in their syntactic expectations should be different, which influences the degree of adaptation for each attachment type. Listeners with LA bias would not need to update their syntactic expectations that much while processing LA sentences (listeners with weaker LA bias may have to update more than those with stronger LA bias), but they may have to update greatly when processing HA sentences (again the degree of update would be different according to the strength of their bias). This process can explain their adaptation toward each type of attachment and greater adaptation toward their less preferred structure (HA) in those with stronger LA bias.

However, eye-tracking data during exposure stage (i.e., data from online adaptation tasks) is more likely to support the error-based learning accounts, rather than the other accounts. The eye-tracking data revealed explicit prediction and prediction error, as expected under the error-based learning accounts. First, depending on their parsing preference (e.g., LA bias) , different degrees of explicit prediction errors were observed at the beginning of each block; their looks to the competitors were significantly greater than looks to the targets at Q1 in the LA block, and at Q1-Q2 in the HA block. While processing their preferred structure, LA, participants showed small degrees of prediction errors at first (Q1) – as some of them could not make correct predictions due to their weak LA bias - and then these prediction errors decreased over the course of the block (Q2-3) with increasing exposure to LA sentences. Ultimately, significant adaptation was found at the end of the block (Q4); their predictive looks at Q4 were significantly different from those at Q1, showing greater looks to the targets.

On the other hand, prediction errors were observed for a longer period of time (Q1 and Q2) while participants were processing their less preferred structure, HA. Then, similarly to the LA block, these prediction errors decreased over time (Q3-4). However, we could not find significant online adaptation effect at the final quartile, but only observed numerical decrease in prediction errors; this may be due to the lengthened prediction errors at the beginning of the HA block. Likewise, the data from online adaptation tasks showed how prediction explicitly changes over time with increasing exposure to a specific structure even though the eye-tracking data from the HA block did not elucidate the entire process of online adaptation toward their less preferred structure. It is likely that there are three main stages for adaptation observed in this study: prediction error (degree differs mainly depending on listeners' parsing bias) – decrease in prediction error – correct prediction aligning with the current linguistic input (adaptation).

As claimed in the error-based learning accounts, participants did show significant adaptation to LA as well as HA after experiencing prediction errors and reducing prediction errors during exposure to each attachment. Reducing prediction errors may reflect the process of weight changes in listeners' current syntactic representations and correct predictions at the end of the LA block may indicate that listeners start to use the changed representations for prediction. This process of adaptation can be explained by the error-based learning accounts as the other accounts did not posit explicit prediction or prediction error in the process of adaptation.

Taken together, this study did not find conclusive evidence that prediction error is manipulated by interaction between individuals' pre-bias and predictive ability, or that adaptation is determined directly by prediction error. However, the findings from this study advanced our understanding of prediction and adaptation. Eye-tracking data during exposure stage shed light on how prediction is made and changed over time when repeatedly encountering a specific construction (e.g., preferred and less preferred structures); listeners explicitly made some degrees of wrong pre-activation about upcoming input depending on their bias at first and then reduced the wrong pre- activation and finally made correct predictions aligning with the input. Then, offline data revealed that listeners could change their preference in interpretations of a particular ambiguity (e.g., RC attachment) and adapt to the current input after experiencing that series of prediction changes.

Likewise, online eye-tracking data combined with offline pre-and post-tests enhanced our understanding of adaptation as they presented a better picture of the entire process of adaptation during and after exposure to a certain structure. The findings of this study that listeners could adapt to the current linguistic input going through a series of changes in their predictions provide further evidence supporting the EBL accounts that posit a close relationship between prediction (error) and adaptation.

Implications for Learning

♦ ♦ ♦

As reviewed earlier, syntactic adaptation has been considered a form of implicit learning and the findings from this study shed light on how implicit learning (adaptation) occurs. In the current study, semantic constraints served as predictive cues. Based on their previous linguistic bias, participants made predictions using these semantic cues and experienced some degrees of prediction errors. Their prediction errors decreased over time as they were encountering more sentences with the same structure. After that, they showed adaptation toward each structure that they were intensively exposed to. This suggests that they could implicitly learn the abstract structure of each attachment type during exposure stage (with no explicit explanation about the rule of structure), and then they imposed the structure when they interpreted ambiguous RC sentences.

Learning abstract structures is considered a challenging task for learners and it has been reported that it takes a long time for speakers to change their abstract, syntactic preferences based on natural exposure. In this line of research, Dussias and Sagarra

(2007) investigated how speakers adjust their language use on the basis of exposure using RC attachment ambiguities (similar to the materials used in this study). Native Spanish speakers are known to be more likely to interpret ambiguous RC sentences in English as HA (preference for HA) because of transfer effect from their first language (L1). However, their preference has been changed to LA after being immersed in an English language environment which can naturally increase their exposure to LA interpretations (note that monolingual English speakers prefer LA).

Importantly, change in their RC attachment preference toward LA was only observed from Spanish speakers who lived in an English speaking country for an average of 7 years, but not from those who had been immersed for an average of 8.5 months. Spanish speakers with an average of 8.5 month-immersion did not differ in their attachment preferences from Spanish speakers with less exposure to English. Given this long time to change one's syntactic preference, significant adaptation toward each attachment type in a short time that we found in this study is very striking and thus has implications for learning. Listeners' adaptation can be much more encouraged when they are given useful cues prompting prediction and prediction error and/ or when they are exposed to a linguistic environment in which they can easily track context-specific syntactic distributions. Taking these into account, we can develop teaching pedagogy or teaching materials, and create learning environments such that learners can implicitly learn syntactic structures or regulations. Further research into various factors that can enhance language users' prediction or mapping between linguistic properties and contextual features can lead to greater understanding on how to encourage implicit learning for abstract syntactic representations.

Limitations

♦ ♦ ♦

The main findings of this study should be interpreted considering manipulation of this study. We exposed participants to their preferred structure first (e.g., LA block), followed by their less preferred structure (e.g., HA block) because participants would come to the lab with their own bias shaped by life-long experiences with RC attachment. Once participants with LA bias are exposed to HA block, their LA bias would potentially be changed as a result of their exposure to HA. Then, what we would measure after their exposure to the LA block followed by the HA block would be their re-adaptation to LA. These people cannot be directly compared with those who are exposed to their preferred structure, LA first (not affected by the other structure, HA).

Another reason for this manipulation was to control for other individual differences that can influence language users' prediction and adaptation. A within-subject design was preferred since our main interest in this study was to investigate whether listeners' adaptation is influenced by their parsing bias and predictive ability (adaptation affected by individual differences). A between-subject design was considered to invite effects of other individual differences on prediction or adaptation, beyond two factors that we were interested in. However, this manipulation could make their LA parsing more activated, causing participants to struggle more during the HA block. To better understand relation between prediction and adaptation, it is necessary to observe adaptation pattern by exposing participants with LA bias to the HA first as well. In addition, for the fair comparison, we need to investigate whether those having HA bias would show the same pattern with those having LA bias when the same manipulation was applied.

Theoretically, prediction error can be determined by degree of individuals' parsing bias interacting with their predictive ability (or sensitivity). However, we could not find any evidence for this hypothesis in the current study and it can be because of limitations in measurement for bias and predictive ability. Individuals can have different bias in terms of RC attachment. In this study, we measured their bias only once using 12 ambiguous RC sentences in this experiment. For more reliable measure, we may consider measuring participants' interpretation in RC attachment ambiguity more than once at different times, if possible with increasing number of sentences, and use averaged value for their bias.

In addition, a more sophisticated methodology seems to be required to measure predictive ability. Visual displays in prediction phase in the current study did not include competitors as we compared fixation proportions on the targets between two conditions. However, this manipulation may allow participants to fixate on targets quite quickly with ease, unlike the conditions in which we used competitors for the adaptation phase. Given that visual displays were presented for 2000 ms before auditory sentences, participants could remember the position of each item and make a quick look at the target items upon hearing the target verbs. This was evidenced in Figure 5-1; their eye fixations on the targets started to diverge between two conditions as soon as they heard the target verbs. In this process, anticipatory looks measuring prediction can be confounded with working memory capacity.

It is possible that those with good (visual) working memory who can remember the positions of items better may throw quick fixations to the target items and fixate them more often during the critical time window for prediction (while listening to verb + the). Therefore, in order to address the question of whether degree of prediction error is manipulated by interaction between individuals' parsing bias and predictive ability, a much more sophisticated methodology is recommended that can measure individuals' bias, prediction and predictive ability.

Future Directions

♦ ♦ ♦

Using More Cues

A factor that should be considered when interpreting these results is that we did not use prosodic cues which can help resolve RC attachment for experimental sentences. We only manipulated semantic cues and we neutralized the prosody of the NP1 and the NP2` and deleted any prosodic boundaries that may have given cues for attachment resolution. This is a limitation of the current study because speakers are known to use prosodic cues to disambiguate ambiguities including RC attachment (Hwang et al., 2011). For example, in a given example sentence like *Someone shot the servant of the actress who was on the balcony,* if a prosodic boundary follows the NP1 (the servant), listeners interpret it as low attachment whereas if a prosodic boundary follows the NP2, listeners interpret it as high attachment. In real language use, prosodic cues are accessible and often facilitate language processing.

Prior prediction studies also revealed that native speakers use prosody for predictions (Nakamura et al., 2012) and that they are able to use redundant cues to maximize the utility of prediction keeping track of their availability (Henry, Hopp, & Jackson, 2017). Therefore, if an additional cue, such as prosodic cue, is imposed onto the sentences, listeners' predictive processing and adaptation can be more encouraged. This question could not be addressed in this study and remains for future studies. Using various cues is important as it mirrors the context of real language use.

Language users may rely on different cues to different extents when various cues are available. Those who showed little predictive ability in the semantically constrained context in this study may depend on prosodic boundaries or other constraints for determining interpretation of RC attachment. Therefore, investigating the effect of different cues on prediction and adaptation in various groups of people is crucial to understand the true relation between prediction and adaptation in real language.

Social Context

The experimental settings of this study did not reflect the real linguistic environment which provides a social and communicative context in which we commonly observe linguistic adaptation at different levels. The possibility that language use in communicative social settings can be at play for adaptation is found in the priming literature. Previous priming studies addressing effects of social factors have shown that priming was greater when interlocutors shared the common goal such as successful communication (Branigan, Pickering, McLean, & Cleland, 2007), or worked together for the same goal (Reitter & Moore, 2014; Reitter, Moore, & Keller, 2006).

Therefore, a social context may be one of the reasons that it is hard to replicate adaptation in the lab settings. Participants in the experiment are not typically required to communicate with others or exposed to social cues, but just to read or listen to isolated sentences. This setting excludes social cues enhancing communication, efficiency of language processing, and adaptation. Future studies including social context are recommended to better understand linguistic adaptation occurring in natural language use.

Memory Consolidation

As pointed above, prediction error was not linearly decreased. Instead, there were some stages with similar fixation proportions to the targets and to the competitors before showing correct predictions. This pattern may reflect time required for changes in context-specific frequency distributions to be stored and consolidated in memory. This thought is in line with the findings from studies observing adaption across multiple sessions. Such studies that allowed time for memory consolidation have reported that adaptation effect could last several days (Wells et al., 2009) to nine months (Kroczek & Gunter, 2017).

Similarly, a recent study on accent adaptation reported that sleep-mediated consolidation could facilitate generalization across accented speakers regardless of phonetic similarities between speakers (Xie, Earle, & Myers, 2018). With absence of social factors in the lab settings, lack of time for memory consolidation may account for the fact that adaptation found in one context of experiments rarely generalizes to another context (e.g., Atkinson et al., 2018).

Truly, in contrast to the lab settings in which participants are exposed to similar stimuli intensively in a short time, listeners in natural language environment encounter specific structures repeatedly over longer stretches of time, which enables them to access and consolidate the stored representations. This process can strengthen the memory representations, promoting generalization of adaptation to specific structures. Thus, in order to better understand adaptation relating to implicit learning, future studies should address this issue, that is, the extent to which memory consolidation influences longevity of adaptation effect and generalization of adaptation.

Individual Differences

Another interesting point that draws our attention was individual variances in prediction and adaptation. The finding that syntactic adaptation was directly influenced by individuals' predictive ability interacting with their bias indicates the importance of predictive ability for adaptation. As seen in results from the prediction phase, while native English speakers overall showed predictive processing, there was considerable variance.

To date, variability has been mainly discussed in developmental studies (children) or bilingual studies (second language speakers). Children's anticipation of upcoming linguistic input is strongly influenced by their vocabulary size (Borovsky et al., 2012), production vocabulary size (Mani & Huettig, 2012) or reading ability (Mani & Huettig, 2014). For second language (L2) speakers, though they have L2 knowledge, they do not show predictive processing, or if they do, it is not to the same extent as native speakers.

It was pointed out that they may lack cognitive resources for predictive processing during L2 processing (See Kaan 2014 for more discussion). Similar to the studies on children and L2 speakers, we found that individual participants' predictive ability greatly varied, and some even did not show any predictive processing though they are adult native English speakers. This may result from using complex sentences (e.g., RC attachment sentences) which can require more cognitive resources. Parallel to studies in different populations, the findings of individual differences in prediction and adaptation leave open the question of which factors make some listeners predict better than others, or adapt more to the current linguistic input than others. Therefore, it is worth exploring the contributing factors to predictive ability, or sensitivity to prediction errors, using various individual differences tasks in different populations. This line of studies may have to use diverse cognitive tasks as well as linguistic tasks. We collected some measures regarding cognitive capacity and linguistic knowledge while conducting the current study and will analyze them later to further understand individual differences in prediction and adaptation.

Conclusion

♦ ♦ ♦

Syntactic adaptation is an important linguistic phenomenon suggesting that change in language processing can be long-lasting and thus linked with language learning. With the aim of better understanding underlying mechanisms of syntactic adaptation, this study tested the hypothesis generated from the error-based learning accounts which emphasize the role of prediction in adaptation. Specifically, we examined whether adaptation is guided by prediction error, presumably from interactions between listeners' parsing bias and predictive ability. We could not find evidence of prediction error modulated by interaction between parsing bias and predictive ability, and the direct link between prediction error and adaptation. Therefore, the questions of whether prediction error leads to adaptation and whether degree of prediction error manipulates magnitude of adaptation remain open for future studies.

However, the findings from this study revealed that listeners make explicit predictions and experience different degrees of prediction errors based on their prior experience. In addition, listeners' prediction errors are reduced with increasing exposure to a specific structure, and ultimately their predictions align with the current linguistic input. After experiencing these series of prediction changes during exposure, listeners are likely to change their interpretations of a particular ambiguity as a function of exposure. These findings partially support the error-based learning accounts and further advanced our understanding of prediction and adaptation. Given that adaptation is related to learning, further investigation on the role of prediction and prediction errors in adaptation will shed light on important factors in implicit learning, contributing to psycholinguistic literature of syntactic adaptation and education literature.

APPENDIX

RESULTS OF NORMING STUDY

◆ ◆ ◆

Table A-1. Norming study 1: Biasing Condition – NP1 Agent

Item	Visual Stimuli	Sentence Fragment	Target (Proportion)	Distractor 1 (Proportion)	Distractor 2 (Proportion
1a NP1		The mother will close the	Jack-in-the-box (96.15%)	Soccer Ball (0.00%)	Doll (3.85%)
2a NP1		The mother will drink the	Milk (100%)	Newspaper (0.00%)	Banana (0.00%)
3a NP1		The girl will dress the	Doll (100%)	Car (0.00%)	Legos (0.00%)
4a NP1		The boy will open the	Present (100%)	Necklace (0.00%)	Money (0.00%)
5a NP1		The father will ride the	Bicycle (100%)	Shovel (0.00%)	Umbrella (0.00%)
6a NP1		The father will bite the	Apple (95.83%)	Phone (4.17%)	Book (0.00%)
7a NP1		The uncle will hunt the	Rabbit (95.83%)	Plant (0.00%)	Car (4.17%)

Table A-1. Continued

8a NP1	 The uncle will throw the	Ball (95.83%)	Backpack (0.00%)	Coffee (4.17%)
9a NP1	 The girl will fly the	Kite (96.15%)	Sandwich (0.00%)	Dress (3.85%)
10a NP1	 The girl will taste the	Chicken (96.15%)	Dog (0.00%)	Flower (3.15%)
11a NP1	 The brother will build the	Snowman (100%)	Tree (0.00%)	River (0.00%)
12a NP1	 The brother will shut the	Box (92.31%)	TV (7.69%)	Bed (0.00%)
13a NP1	 The girl will make the	Paper Airplane (80.00%)	Treasure Chest (12.00%)	Pencil (8.00%)
14a NP1	 The girl will write the	Letter (92.00%)	Gift (4.00%)	Picture Frame (4.00%)
15a NP1	 The teacher will read the	Book (96.00%)	Door (0.00%)	Ruler (4.00%)
16a NP1	 The teacher will drive the	Car (96.00%)	Hammock (0.00%)	Tent (4.00%)

Table A-2. Norming study 1: Biasing Condition – NP2 Agent

Item	Visual Stimuli	Sentence Fragment	Target (Proportion)	Distractor 1 (Proportion)	Distractor 2 (Proportion)
1a NP2		The boy will close the	Jack-in-the-box (95.83%)	Soccer Ball (4.17%)	Doll (0.00%)
2a NP2		The boy will drink the	Milk (100%)	Newspaper (0.00%)	Banana (0.00%)
3a NP2		The dancer will dress the	Doll (95.83%)	Car (0.00%)	Legos (4.17%)
4a NP2		The dancer will open the	Present (100%)	Necklace (0.00%)	Money (0.00%)
5a NP2		The boy will ride the	Bicycle (96.15%)	Shovel (0.00%)	Umbrella (3.85%)
6a NP2		The boy will bite the	Apple (92.31%)	Phone (3.85%)	Book (3.85%)
7a NP2		The boy will hunt the	Rabbit (92.31%)	Plant (7.69%)	Car (0.00%)
8a NP2		The boy will throw the	Ball (96.15%)	Backpack (0.00%)	Coffee (3.85%)
9a NP2		The boy will fly the	Kite (92.00%)	Sandwich (4.00%)	Dress (4.00%)

Table A-2. Continued

10a NP2		The boy will taste the	Chicken (92.00%)	Dog (8.00%)	Flower (0.00%)
11a NP2		The girl will build the	Snowman (92.00%)	Tree (4.00%)	River (4.00%)
12a NP2		The girl will shut the	Box (80.00%)	TV (12.00%)	Bed (8.00%)
13a NP2		The boy will make the	Paper Airplane (92.31%)	Treasure Chest (7.69%)	Pencil (0.00%)
14a NP2	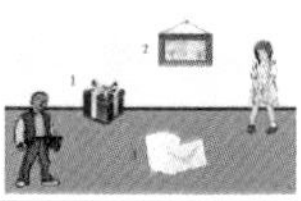	The boy will write the	Letter (100%)	Gift (0.00%)	Picture (0.00%)
15a NP2		The student will read the	Book (96.15%)	Door (3.85%)	Ruler (0.00%)
16a NP2		The student will drive the	Car (100%)	Hammock (0.00%)	Tent (0.00%)

Table A-3. Norming study 1: Neutral Condition – NP1 Agent

Item	Visual Stimuli	Sentence Fragment	Target (Proportion)	Distractor 1 (Proportion)	Distractor 2 (Proportion
1b NP1		The mother will move the	Jack-in-the-box (46.15%)	Soccer Ball (38.46%)	Doll (15.38%)
2b NP1		The mother will drop the	Milk (26.92%)	Newspaper (3.85%)	Banana (69.23 %)
3b NP1		The girl will bring the	Doll (65.38%)	Car (19.23%)	Legos (15.38%)
4b NP1		The boy will get the	Present (76.92%)	Necklace (3.85%)	Money (19.23%)
5b NP1		The father will need the	Bicycle (16.00%)	Shovel (64.00%)	Umbrella (20.00%)
6b NP1		The father will have the	Apple (56.00%)	Phone (40.00%)	Book (4.00%)
7b NP1		The uncle will touch the	Rabbit (68.00%)	Plant (8.00%)	Car (24.00%)
8b NP1		The uncle will take the	Ball (28.00%)	Backpack (16.00%)	Coffee (56.00%)
9b NP1		The girl will pick the	Kite (26.92%)	Sandwich (23.08 %)	Dress (50.00%)

Table A-3. Continued

10b NP1		The girl will like the	Chicken (15.38%)	Dog (30.77%)	Flower (53.85%)
11b NP1		The brother will see the	Snowman (80.77%)	Tree (11.54%)	River (7.69%)
12b NP1		The brother will want the	Box (11.54%)	TV (76.92%)	Bed (11.54%)
13b NP1		The girl will find the	Paper Airplane (8.33%)	Treasure Chest (91.67%)	Pencil (0.00%)
14b NP1		The girl will keep the	Letter (25.00%)	Gift (70.83%)	Picture Frame (4.17%)
15b NP1		The teacher will hold the	Book (50.00%)	Door (8.33%)	Ruler (41.67%)
16b NP1		The teacher will buy the	Car (79.17%)	Hammock (8.33%)	Tent (12.50%)

Table A-4. Norming study 1: Neutral Condition - NP2 Agent

Item	Visual Stimuli	Sentence Fragment	Target (Proportion)	Distractor 1 (Proportion)	Distractor 2 (Proportion)
1b NP2		The boy will move the	Jack-in-the-box (8.00%)	Soccer Ball (80.00%)	Doll (12.00%)
2b NP2		The boy will drop the	Milk (32.00%)	Newspaper (32.00%)	Banana (36.00%)
3b NP2		The dancer will bring the	Doll (76.00%)	Car (20.00%)	Legos (4.00%)
4b NP2		The dancer will get the	Present (28.00%)	Necklace (36.00%)	Money (36.00%)
5b NP2		The boy will need the	Bicycle (69.23%)	Shovel (3.85%)	Umbrella (26.92%)
6b NP2		The boy will have the	Apple (65.38%)	Phone (23.08%)	Book (11.54%)
7b NP2		The boy will touch the	Rabbit (61.54%)	Plant (26.92%)	Car (11.54%)
8b NP2		The boy will take the	Ball (30.77%)	Backpack (69.23%)	Coffee (0.00%)
9b NP2		The boy will pick the	Kite (37.50%)	Sandwich (54.17%)	Dress (8.33%)

Table A-4. Continued

10b NP2		The boy will like the	Chicken (25.00%)	Dog (75.00%)	Flower (0.00%)
11b NP2		The girl will see the	Snowman (58.33%)	Tree (16.67%)	River (25.00%)
12b NP2		The girl will want the	Box (25.00%)	TV (41.67%)	Bed (33.33%)
13b NP2	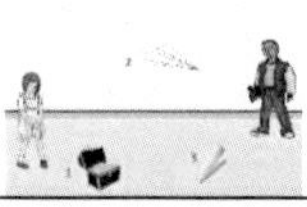	The boy will find the	Paper Airplane (7.69%)	Treasure Chest (76.92%)	Pencil (15.38%)
14b NP2		The boy will keep the	Letter (11.54%)	Gift (80.77%)	Picture (7.69%)
15b NP2		The student will hold the	Book (61.54%)	Door (19.23%)	Ruler (19.23%)
16b NP2		The student will buy the	Car (73.08%)	Hammock (11.54%)	Tent (15.38%)

Table A-5. Norming study 1: Adaptation - NP1

Item	Visual Stimuli	Sentence Fragment	Target	Competitor	Distractor 1	Distractor 2
1a NP1		The uncle will ride the	Motorcycle (84.31%)	Rocking Horse (11.76%)	Tuba (3.92%)	Pinwheel (0.00%)
2a NP1		The master will bury the	Treasure Chest (80.39%)	Bone (15.69%)	Lake (3.92%)	Coffee (0.00%)
3a NP1		The master will chew the	Gum (88.24%)	Stick (3.92%)	Fish (5.88%)	Ball (1.96%)
4a NP1		The owner will climb the	Mountain (88.24%)	Cat House (7.84%)	Mouse (1.96%)	Orange (1.96%)
5a NP1		The owner will eat the	Cake (98.04%)	Lizard (1.96%)	Collar (0.00%)	Shoes (0.00%)
6a NP1		The husband will push the	Lawn Mower (88.24%)	Stroller (11.76%)	Tool Box (0.00%)	Suitcase (0.00%)
7a NP1		The father will read the	Blueprints (74.51%)	Book (25.49%)	House (0.00%)	Sand Castle (0.00%)
8a NP1		The tailor will cut the	Fabric (96.00%)	Pipe (2.00%)	Sink (0.00%)	Sewing Machine (2.00%)
9a NP1		The coach will carry the	Clipboard (44.00%)	Toys (6.00%)	Bubbles (2.00%)	Whistle (48.00%)

Table A-5. Continued

10a NP1		The uncle will sail the	Ship (0.00%)	Toy boat (0.00%)	Pail (0.00%)	Fishing Rod (0.00%)
11a NP1		The uncle will sip the	Wine (94.00%)	Juice (6.00%)	Fox (0.00%)	Target (0.00%)
12a NP1		The owner will taste the	Watermel on (98.00%)	Dog Food (2.00%)	Dog House (0.00%)	Bed (0.00%)
13a NP1		The uncle will ride the	Mechanic al Bull (96.00%)	Carousel (4.00%)	Newspap er (0.00%)	Book (0.00%)
14a NP1		The wife will wear the	Dress (86.00%)	Suit (2.00%)	Broken Shoes (12.00%)	Broken Watch (0.00%)
15a NP1		The uncle will carry the	First-aid Kit (98.00%)	Teddy bear (0.00%)	Tank (2.00%)	Toy Car (0.00%)
1e NP1		The uncle will blow the	Tuba (94.12%)	Pinwheel (0.00%)	Motorcycl e (1.96%)	Rocking Horse (3.92%)
2e NP1		The master will drink the	Coffee (96.08%)	Lake (3.92%)	Treasure Chest (0.00%)	Bone (0.00%)
3e NP1		The master will chase the	Fish (60.78%)	Ball (31.37%)	Gum (0.00%)	Stick (7.84%)

Table A-5. Continued

4e NP1		The owner will eat the	Orange (96.08%)	Mouse (1.96%)	Mountain (0.00%)	Cat House (1.96%)
5e NP1		The owner will wear the	Shoes (100%)	Collar (0.00%)	Lizard (0.00%)	Cake (0.00%)
6e NP1		The husband will close the	Toolbox (84.31%)	Suitcase (11.76%)	Lawn Mower (0.00%)	Stroller (3.92%)
7e NP1		The father will build the	House (84.31%)	Sand Castle (13.73%)	Blueprint s (1.96%)	Book (0.00%)
8e NP1		The tailor will repair the	Sewing Machine (62.00%)	Sink (12.00%)	Cloth (22.00%)	Pipe (4.00%)
9e NP1		The coach will blow the	Whistle (100%)	Bubbles (0.00%)	Toys (0.00%)	Clipboard (0.00%)
10e NP1		The uncle will use the	Fishing rod (70.00%)	Pail (0.00%)	Ship (26.00%)	Toy boat (4.00%)
11e NP1		The uncle will shoot the	Fox (74.00%)	Target (24.00%)	Juice (0.00%)	Wine (0.00%)
12e NP1		The owner will use the	Bed (92.00%)	Dog House (4.00%)	Watermel on (4.00%)	Dog Food (0.00%)

Table A-5. Continued

13e NP1		The uncle will read the	Newspaper (90.00%)	Book (8.00%)	Carousel (2.00%)	Mechanical Bull (0.00%)
14e NP1		The wife will repair the	Broken Necklace (56.00%)	Broken Watch (34.00%)	Dress (10.00%)	Suit (0.00%)
15e NP1		The uncle will drive the	Tank (96.00%)	Toy car (4.00%)	First-aid Kit (0.00%)	Teddy Bear (0.00%)

Table A-6. Norming study 1: Adaptation – NP2

Item	Visual Stimuli	Sentence Fragment	Target	Competitor	Distractor 1	Distractor 2
1b NP2		The girl will ride the	Rocking Horse (98.00%)	Motorcycle (2.00%)	Tuba (0.00%)	Pinwheel (0.00%)
2b NP2		The dog will bury the	Bone (96.00%)	Treasure (4.00%)	Lake (0.00%)	Coffee (0.00%)
3b NP2		The puppy will chew the	Stick (50.00%)	Gum (2.00%)	Fish (0.00%)	Ball (48.00%)
4b NP2		The cat will climb the	Cat House (94.00%)	Mountain (6.00%)	Mouse (0.00%)	Orange (0.00%)
5b NP2		The cat will eat the	Lizard (66.00%)	Cake (34.00%)	Collar (0.00%)	Shoes (0.00%)
6b NP2		The wife will push the	Stroller (76.00%)	Lawnmower (24.00%)	Toolbox (0.00%)	Suitcase (0.00%)
7b NP2		The boy will read the	Book (94.00%)	Blueprints (4.00%)	House (0.00%)	Sandcastle (2.00%)
8b NP2		The plumber will cut the	Pipe (88.24%)	Fabric (3.92%)	Sink (5.88%)	Sewing Machine (1.96%)
9b NP2		The boy will carry the	Toys (47.06%)	Clipboard (13.73%)	Bubbles (29.41%)	Whistle (9.80%)

Table A-6. Continued

10b NP2	The boy will sail the	Toy boat (68.63%)	Ship (27.45%)	Pail (0.00%)	Fishing Rod (3.92%)
11b NP2	The boy will sip the	Juice (86.27%)	Wine (9.80%)	Fox (1.96%)	Target (1.96%)
12b NP2	The dog will taste the	Dog food (96.08%)	Watermelon (0.00%)	Dog House (1.96%)	Bed (1.96%)
13b NP2	The girl will ride the	Carousel (64.71%)	Mechanical Bull (33.33%)	Newspaper (1.96%)	Book (0.00%)
14b NP2	The man will wear the	Suit (94.12%)	Dress (1.96%)	Broken Necklace (1.96%)	Broken Watch (1.96%)
15b NP2	The boy will carry the	Teddy Bear (80.39%)	First-aid Kit (9.80%)	Tank (0.00%)	Toy Car (9.80%)
1f NP2	The girl will blow the	Pinwheel (56.00%)	Tuba (44.00%)	Motorcycle (0.00%)	Rocking Horse (0.00%)
2f NP2	The dog will drink the	Lake (92.00%)	Coffee (8.00%)	Treasure Chest (0.00%)	Bone (0.00%)
3f NP2	The puppy will chase the	Ball (76.00%)	Fish (2.00%)	Stick (22.00%)	Gum (0.00%)

Table A-6. Continued

4f NP2		The cat will eat the	Mouse (94.00%)	Orange (6.00%)	Mountain (0.00%)	Cat House (0.00%)
5f NP2		The cat will wear the	Collar (96.00%)	Shoes (0.00%)	Lizard (2.00%)	Cake (0.00%)
6f NP2		The wife will close the	Suitcase (88.00%)	Toolbox (12.00%)	Lawnmower (0.00%)	Stroller (0.00%)
7f NP2		The boy will build the	Sand Castle (98.00%)	House (2.00%)	Blueprints (0.00%)	Book (0.00%)
8f NP2		The plumber will repair the	Sink (88.24%)	Sewing Machine (1.96%)	Fabric (0.00%)	Pipe (9.80%)
9f NP2		The boy will blow the	Bubbles (47.06%)	Whistle (49.02%)	Toys (1.96%)	Clipboard (1.96%)
10f NP2		The boy will use the	Pail (72.55%)	Fishing Rod (25.49%)	Ship (0.00%)	Toy Boat (1.96%)
11f NP2		The boy will shoot the	Target (86.27%)	Fox (9.80%)	Juice (1.96%)	Wine (1.96%)
12f NP2		The dog will use the	Dog House (76.47%)	Bed (1.96%)	Watermelon (3.92%)	Dog Food (17.65%)

Table A-6. Continued

13f NP2		The girl will read the	Book (70.59%)	Newspaper (25.49%)	Carousel (0.00%)	Mechanical Bull (3.92%)
14f NP2		The man will repair the	Broken Watch (88.24%)	Broken Necklace (11.76%)	Dress (0.00%)	Suit (0.00%)
15f NP2		The boy will drive the	Toy car (88.24%)	Tank (9.80%)	First-aid Kit (1.96%)	Teddy Bear (0.00%)

Table A-7. Norming study 2: Biasing Condition - NP1 Agent

Item	Visual Stimuli	Sentence Fragment	Target (Proportion)	Distractor 1 (Proportion)	Distractor 2 (Proportion
1a NP1		The mother will close the	Jack-in-the-box (96.15%)	Soccer Ball (3.85%)	Train (0.00%)
2a NP1		The mother will drink the	Milk (100%)	Newspaper (0.00%)	Banana (0.00%)
3a NP1		The girl will dress the	Doll (100%)	Purse (0.00%)	Legos (0.00%)
4a NP1		The boy will open the	Present (100%)	Trophy (0.00%)	Money (0.00%)
5a NP1		The father will ride the	Bicycle (95.83%)	Shovel (0.00%)	Umbrella (4.17%)
6a NP1		The father will bite the	Apple (95.83%)	Phone (4.17%)	Book (0.00%)
7a NP1		The uncle will hunt the	Rabbit (95.83%)	Plant (0.00%)	Car (4.17%)
8a NP1		The uncle will throw the	Ball (91.67%)	Backpack (0.00%)	Coffee (8.33%)
9a NP1		The girl will fly the	Kite (95.83%)	Sandwich (0.00%)	Dress (4.17%)

Table A-7. Continued

10a NP1		The girl will taste the	Chicken (95.83%)	Dog (0.00%)	Kite (4.17%)
11a NP1		The brother will build the	Snowman (100%)	Tree (0.00%)	Shovel (0.00%)
12a NP1		The brother will shut the	Box (100%)	Chair (0.00%)	Bed (0.00%)
13a NP1	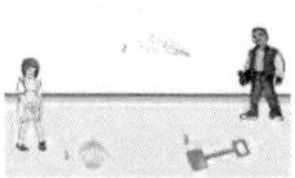	The girl will make the	Paper Airplane (85.19%)	Shell (11.11%)	Shovel (3.70%)
14a NP1		The girl will write the	Letter (88.89%)	Receipt (7.41%)	Present (3.70%)
15a NP1		The teacher will read the	Book (100%)	Pencil (0.00%)	Ruler (0.00%)
16a NP1		The teacher will drive the	Car (92.59%)	Hammock (7.41%)	Tent (0.00%)

Table A-8. Norming study 2: Biasing Condition - NP2 Agent

Item	Visual Stimuli	Sentence Fragment	Target (Proportion)	Distractor 1 (Proportion)	Distractor 2 (Proportion)
1a NP2		The boy will close the	Jack-in-the-box (95.83%)	Soccer Ball (4.17%)	Doll (0.00%)
2a NP2		The boy will drink the	Milk (100%)	Newspaper (0.00%)	Banana (0.00%)
3a NP2		The dancer will dress the	Doll (100%)	Car (0.00%)	Legos (0.00%)
4a NP2		The dancer will open the	Present (100%)	Necklace (0.00%)	Money (0.00%)
5a NP2		The boy will ride the	Bicycle (95.83%)	Water Bottle (4.17%)	Cap (0.00%)
6a NP2		The boy will bite the	Apple (95.83%)	Phone (0.00%)	Cap (4.17%)
7a NP2		The boy will hunt the	Rabbit (95.83%)	Plant (0.00%)	Cat (4.17%)
8a NP2		The boy will throw the	Ball (100%)	Backpack (0.00%)	Water Bottle (0.00%)
9a NP2		The boy will fly the	Kite (100%)	Sandwich (0.00%)	Dress (0.00%)

Table A-8. Continued

10a NP2		The boy will taste the	Chicken (100%)	Dog (0.00%)	Kite (0.00%)
11a NP2		The girl will build the	Snowman (100%)	Tree (0.00%)	Shovel (0.00%)
12a NP2		The girl will shut the	Box (88.89%)	Chair (0.00%)	Bed (11.11%)
13a NP2		The boy will make the	Paper Airplane (92.31%)	Treasure Chest (3.85%)	Pencil (3.85%)
14a NP2		The boy will write the	Letter (100%)	Gift (0.00%)	Picture (0.00%)
15a NP2		The student will read the	Book (96.15%)	Pencil (3.85%)	Ruler (0.00%)
16a NP2		The student will drive the	Car (96.15%)	Hammock (3.85%)	Tent (0.00%)

Table A-9. Norming study 2: Neutral Condition – NP1 Agent

Item	Visual Stimuli	Sentence Fragment	Target (Proportion)	Distractor 1 (Proportion)	Distractor 2 (Proportion)
1b NP1		The mother will move the	Jack-in-the-box (29.17%)	Soccer Ball (33.33%)	Doll (37.50%)
2b NP1		The mother will drop the	Milk (25.00%)	Newspaper (58.33%)	Banana (16.67 %)
3b NP1		The girl will bring the	Doll (70.83%)	Purse (16.67%)	Legos (12.50%)
4b NP1		The boy will get the	Present (37.50%)	Trophy (62.50%)	Money (0.00%)
5b NP1		The father will need the	Bicycle (25.93%)	Water Bottle (59.26%)	Cap (14.81%)
6b NP1		The father will have the	Apple (51.85%)	Phone (40.74%)	Cap (7.41%)
7b NP1		The uncle will touch the	Rabbit (37.04%)	Plant (11.11%)	Cat (51.85%)
8b NP1		The uncle will take the	Ball (22.22%)	Backpack (18.52%)	Water Bottle (59.26%)
9b NP1		The girl will pick the	Kite (30.77%)	Sandwich (23.08 %)	Dress (46.15%)

Table A-9. Continued

10b NP1	 The girl will like the	Chicken (7.69%)	Dog (61.54%)	Kite (30.77%)
11b NP1	 The brother will see the	Snowman (80.77%)	Tree (15.38%)	Shovel (3.85%)
12b NP1	 The brother will want the	Box (57.69%)	Chair (7.69%)	Bed (34.62%)
13b NP1	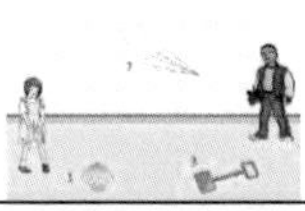 The girl will find the	Paper Airplane (4.17%)	Shell (95.83%)	Pencil (0.00%)
14b NP1	 The girl will keep the	Letter (4.17%)	Gift (33.33%)	Picture Frame (62.50%)
15b NP1	 The teacher will hold the	Book (41.67%)	Pencil (20.83%)	Ruler (37.50%)
16b NP1	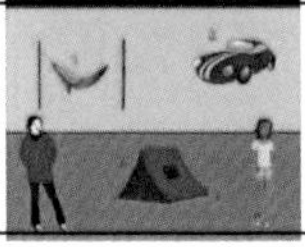 The teacher will buy the	Car (91.67%)	Hammock (4.17%)	Tent (4.17%)

Table A-10. Norming study 2: Neutral Condition – NP2 Agent

Item	Visual Stimuli	Sentence Fragment	Target (Proportion)	Distractor 1 (Proportion)	Distractor 2 (Proportion)
1b NP2		The boy will move the	Jack-in-the-box (3.70%)	Soccer Ball (11.11%)	Train (85.19%)
2b NP2		The boy will drop the	Milk (59.26%)	Newspaper (11.11%)	Banana (29.63%)
3b NP2		The dancer will bring the	Doll (25.93%)	Purse (66.67%)	Legos (7.41%)
4b NP2		The dancer will get the	Present (3.70%)	Trophy (96.30%)	Money (0.00%)
5b NP2		The boy will need the	Bicycle (23.08%)	Water Bottle (61.54%)	Cap (15.38%)
6b NP2		The boy will have the	Apple (53.85%)	Phone (11.54%)	Cap (34.62%)
7b NP2		The boy will touch the	Rabbit (38.46%)	Plant (7.69%)	Cat (53.85%)
8b NP2		The boy will take the	Ball (15.38%)	Backpack (73.08%)	Water Bottle (11.54%)
9b NP2		The boy will pick the	Kite (50.00%)	Sandwich (37.50%)	Dress (12.50%)

Table A-10. Continued

10b NP2		The boy will like the	Chicken (25.00%)	Dog (50.00%)	Kite (25.00%)
11b NP2		The girl will see the	Snowman (58.33%)	Tree (37.50%)	Shovel (4.17%)
12b NP2		The girl will want the	Box (37.50%)	Chair (12.50%)	Bed (50.00%)
13b NP2	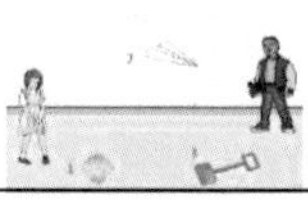	The boy will find the	Paper Airplane (8.33%)	Shell (87.50%)	Shovel (4.17%)
14b NP2		The boy will keep the	Letter (4.17%)	Gift (45.83%)	Receipt (50.00%)
15b NP2		The student will hold the	Book (16.67%)	Pencil (83.33%)	Ruler (0.00 %)
16b NP2	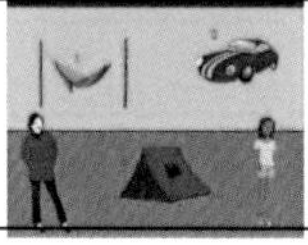	The student will buy the	Car (62.50%)	Hammock (4.17%)	Tent (33.33%)

Table A-11. Norming study 2: Adaptation List – NP1 Agent

Item	Visual Stimuli	Sentence Fragment	Target	Competitor	Distractor 1	Distractor 2
A1a NP1		The uncle will ride the	Motorcycle (96.15%)	Rocking Horse (3.85%)	Tuba (0.00%)	Flowers (0.00%)
A3a NP1		The owner will chew the	Gum (92.31%)	Stick (3.85%)	Polar Bear (0.00%)	Ball (3.85%)
A5a NP1		The owner will eat the	Cake (92.31%)	Lizard (3.85%)	Collar (0.00%)	Shoes (3.85%)
A7a NP1		The father will read the	Blueprints (80.77%)	Book (15.38%)	House (3.85%)	Sand Castle (0.00%)
A9a NP1		The man will use the	Treadmill (95.83%)	Crayon (0.00%)	Whistle (4.17%)	Bubble (0.00%)
A10a NP1		The uncle will sail the	Ship (95.83%)	Toy Boat (0.00%)	Pail (4.17%)	Fishing Rod (0.00%)
A11a NP1		The uncle will sip the	Wine (87.50%)	Juice (8.33%)	Fox (4.17%)	Target (0.00%)
A12a NP1		The owner will taste the	Chocolate (95.83%)	Dog Food (0.00%)	Dog House (0.00%)	Bed (4.17%)
A13a NP1		The uncle will ride the	Mechanical Bull (91.67%)	Carousel (4.17%)	Newspaper (4.17%)	Book (0.00%)

Table A-11. Continued

A14a NP1		The wife will wear the	Dress (87.50%)	Suit (4.17%)	Broken Shoes (8.33%)	Broken Watch (0.00%)
A1e NP1		The uncle will blow the	Tuba (100%)	Flower (0.00%)	Motorcycle (0.00%)	Rocking Horse (0.00%)
A3e NP1		The master will chase the	Polar Bear (79.17%)	Ball (20.83%)	Gum (0.00%)	Stick (0.00%)
A5e NP1		The owner will wear the	Shoes (95.83%)	Collar (4.17%)	Cake (0.00%)	Lizard (0.00%)
A7e NP1		The father will build the	House (95.83%)	Sand Castle (4.17%)	Blueprints (0.00%)	Book (0.00%)
A9e NP1		The man will blow the	Whistle (88.89%)	Bubbles (7.41%)	Crayon (0.00%)	Treadmill (3.70%)
A10e NP1		The uncle will use the	Fishing Rod (59.26%)	Pail (0.00%)	Ship (37.04%)	Toy Boat (3.70%)
A11e NP1		The uncle will shoot the	Fox (48.15%)	Target (48.15%)	Juice (3.70%)	Wine (0.00%)
A12e NP1		The owner will use the	Bed (88.89%)	Dog House (3.70%)	Chocolate (7.41%)	Dog Food (0.00%)

Table A-11. Continued

A13e NP1		The uncle will ride the	Mechanical Bull (88.89%)	Carousel (3.70%)	Newspaper (0.00%)	Book (7.41%)
A14e NP1		The wife will repair the	Shoes (59.26%)	Watch (29.63%)	Dress (0.00%)	Suit (11.11%)

Table A-12. Norming study 2: Adaptation List – NP2 Agent

Item	Visual Stimuli	Sentence Fragment	Target	Competitor	Distractor 1	Distractor 2
A1b NP2		The girl will ride the	Rocking Horse (91.67%)	Motorcycle (4.17%)	Tuba (0.00%)	Flower (4.17%)
A3b NP2		The puppy will chew the	Stick (75.00%)	Gum (0.00%)	Polar Bear (0.00%)	Ball (25.00%)
A5b NP2		The cat will eat the	Lizard (62.50%)	Cake (37.50%)	Collar (0.00%)	Shoes (0.00%)
A7b NP2		The boy will read the	Book (91.67%)	Blueprints (8.33%)	House (0.00%)	Sand Castle (0.00%)
A9b NP2		The boy will use the	Crayon (34.62%)	Treadmill (11.54%)	Whistle (11.54%)	Bubbles (38.46%)
A10b NP2		The boy will sail the	Toy boat (76.92%)	Ship (19.23%)	Pail (0.00%)	Fishing Rod (3.85%)
A11b NP2		The boy will sip the	Juice (92.86%)	Wine (0.00%)	Fox (0.00%)	Target (7.14%)
A12b NP2		The dog will taste the	Dog Food (84.00%)	Chocolate (8.00%)	Dog House (4.00%)	Bed (4.00%)
A13b NP2		The girl will ride the	Carousel (76.92%)	Mechanical Bull (19.23%)	Newspaper (3.85%)	Book (0.00%)

Table A-12. Continued

A14b NP2		The man will wear the	Suit (96.15%)	Dress (3.85%)	Broken Shoes (0.00%)	Broken Watch (0.00%)
A1f NP2		The girl will blow the	Flowers (18.52%)	Tuba (81.48%)	Motorcycle (0.00%)	Rocking Horse (0.00%)
A3f NP2		The puppy will chase the	Ball (51.85%)	Polar Bear (7.41%)	Stick (40.74%)	Gum (0.00%)
A5f NP2		The cat will wear the	Collar (96.15%)	Shoes (3.85%)	Cake (0.00%)	Lizard (0.00%)
A7f NP2		The boy will build the	Sand Castle (96.30%)	House (0.00%)	Blueprints (0.00%)	Book (3.70%)
A9f NP2		The boy will blow the	Bubbles (45.83%)	Whistle (54.17%)	Crayon (0.00%)	Treadmill (0.00%)
A10f NP2		The boy will use the	Pail (37.50%)	Fishing Rod (54.17%)	Ship (0.00%)	Toy Boat (8.33%)
A11f NP2		The boy will shoot the	Target (83.33%)	Fox (16.67%)	Juice (0.00%)	Wine (0.00%)
A12f NP2		The dog will use the	Dog House (70.83%)	Bed (4.17%)	Chocolate (0.00%)	Dog Food (25.00%)

Table A-12. Continued

A13f NP2		The uncle will read the	Newspaper (91.67%)	Book (8.33%)	Carousel (0.00%)	Mechanical Bull (0.00%)
A14f NP2		The man will repair the	Broken Watch (91.67%)	Broken Shoes (8.33%)	Dress (0.00%)	Suit (0.00%)

MATERIALS FOR PREDICTION PHASE

◆ ◆ ◆

Table B-1. Experimental sentences for the Biasing condition

I see the mother of the boy that will close the jack-in-the-box.
I see the mother of the boy that will drink the milk
I know the friend of the dancer that will dress the doll
I know the friend of the dancer that will open the present
I meet the father of the boy that will ride the bike
I meet the father of the boy that will bite the apple
I see the uncle of the boy that will hunt the rabbit
I see the uncle of the boy that will throw the ball
I know the friend of the boy that will fly the kite
I know the friend of the boy that will taste the chicken
I meet the brother of the girl that will build the snowman
I see the cousin of the boy that will make the paper airplane
I see the cousin of the boy that will write the letter
I know the teacher of the student that will read the book

Table B-2. Experimental sentences for the Neutral condition

I see the mother of the boy that will move the jack-in-the-box.
I see the mother of the boy that will drop the milk
I know the friend of the dancer that will bring the doll
I know the friend of the dancer that will get the present
I meet the father of the boy that will need the bike
I meet the father of the boy that will take the apple
I see the uncle of the boy that will touch the rabbit
I see the uncle of the boy that will have the ball
I know the friend of the boy that will pick the kite
I know the friend of the boy that will like the chicken
I meet the brother of the girl that will see the snowman
I see the cousin of the boy that will find the paper airplane
I see the cousin of the boy that will keep the letter
I know the teacher of the student that will hold the book

MATERIALS FOR THE OFFLINE ADAPTATION TASK

♦ ♦ ♦

Table C-1. Experimental sentences for pre-and post-tests

Frank meets the author of the editor that is from London.
Michelle sees the child of the mother that is talking to the woman.
Sue knows the master of the servant that is eating a sandwich.
Ben meets the employer of the worker that is very friendly.
Nick sees the student of the tutor that is feeling exhausted.
David knows the pilot of the passenger that is waving his hand.
Sam meets the wife of the husband that is drinking coffee.
Ellen sees the director of the actor that is dreaming of fame.
Kim meets the assistant of the boss that is looking happy.
John sees the visitor of the host that is working hard.
Harry knows the manager of the actress that is wearing jeans.
I meet the client of the hairdresser that is talking loudly.
Isabel sees the aunt of the girl that is sitting down.
Jenny knows the guide of the tourist that is looking energetic.
Sam meets the waitress of the customer that is very talkative.

Kelly sees the soldier of the captain that is reading the book.

Bob knows the father of the boy that is sitting down.

Wilma meets the traveler of the guide that is crossing the river.

Marion sees the nurse of the lawyer that is very kind.

Nate knows the employee of the president that is walking outside.

Todd meets the boss of the secretary that is reading a book.

Olivia sees the coach of the player that is looking confident.

Paul knows the student of the teacher that is very intelligent.

Taylor meets the neighbor of the farmer that is painting the fence.

Bennett sees the child of the woman that is singing on the bench.

Cory knows the follower of the pastor that is praying at church.

Kennedy meets the babysitter of the child that is watching tv.

Drake sees the assistant of the dentist that is working in the office.

Sherry knows the owner of the horse that is eating an apple.

Kenny meets the driver of the CEO that is waiting outside.

Rebecca sees the principal of the student that is eating lunch.

Russel knows the father of the bride that is dancing on the stage.

Laura meets the lawyer of the client that is in the room.

Allen sees the gardener of the doctor that is talking to the lawyer.

Jill knows the chief of the police officer that is sitting at the desk.

MATERIALS FOR THE ONLINE ADAPTATION TASK 1 (LA BLOCK)

♦ ♦ ♦

Table D-1. Experimental sentences in the LA block

I see the uncle of the girl that will ride the rocking horse
I know the niece of the man that will ride the motorbike
That is the uncle of the girl that will blow the pinwheel
I see the niece of the man that will blow the tuba
I know the master of the dog that will bury the bone
That is the dog of the pirate that will bury the treasure
That is the master of the dog that will drink the water
I see the dog of the pirate that will drink the coffee
That is the owner of the puppy that will chew the stick
I see the puppy of the Eskimo that will chew the gum
That is the owner of the puppy that will chase the ball
That is the puppy of the Eskimo that will chase the polar bear
I see the owner of the cat that will climb the cat tower
That is the cat of the man that will climb the mountain
I see the owner of the cat that will eat the mouse

I see the cat of the man that will eat the bread

That is the owner of the cat that will eat the lizard

That is the cat of the woman that will eat the cake

I know the owner of the cat that will wear the collar

I know the cat of the woman that will wear the shoes

That is the husband of the wife that will push the stroller

That is the woman of the man that will push the lawn mower

I see the husband of the wife that will close the suitcase

That is the woman of the man that will close the tool box

That is the father of the boy that will read the book

I know the son of the builder that will read the plans

I know the father of the boy that will build the sand castle

I see the son of the builder that will build the house

That is the friend of the plumber that will cut the pipe

I see the friend of the tailor that will cut the fabric

I know the friend of the plumber that will repair the sink

I see the friend of the tailor that will repair the sewing machine

I see the father of the child that will use the tricycle

That is the son of the father that will use the treadmill

That is the father of the child that will blow the bubble

I know the son of the father that will blow the whistle

I know the uncle of the boy that will sip the juice

That is the cousin of the hunter that will sip the wine

I see the uncle of the boy that will shoot the archery target

That is the cousin of the hunter that will shoot the fox

I know the owner of the dog that will taste the dog food

I see the dog of the boy that will taste the chocolate

I see the owner of the dog that will use the doghouse

That is the dog of the boy that will use the bed

I know the uncle of the girl that will ride the carousel

I see the niece of the cowboy that will ride the bull

I know the uncle of the girl that will read the book

I know the niece of the cowboy that will read the newspaper

I see the wife of the man that will wear the suit

I see the husband of the woman that will wear the dress

That is the wife of the man that will repair the watch

That is the husband of the woman that will repair the shoe

I see the uncle of the boy that will carry the teddy bear

That is the nephew of the soldier that will carry the first aid

That is the uncle of the boy that will drive the toy car

I know the nephew of the soldier that will drive the tank

MATERIALS FOR THE ONLINE ADAPTATION TASK 2 (HA BLOCK)

♦ ♦ ♦

Table E-1. Experimental sentences in the HA block

I know the uncle of the girl that will ride the motorbike
That is the niece of the man that will ride the rocking horse
I see the uncle of the girl that will blow the tuba
I know the niece of the man that will blow the pinwheel
That is the master of the dog that will bury the treasure
I see the dog of the pirate that will bury the bone
I know the master of the dog that will drink the coffee
That is the dog of the pirate that will drink the water
I see the owner of the puppy that will chew the gum
I know the puppy of the Eskimo that will chew the stick
I know the owner of the puppy that will chase the polar bear
I see the puppy of the Eskimo that will chase the ball
I know the owner of the cat that will climb the mountain
I know the cat of the man that will climb the cat tower
That is the owner of the cat that will eat the bread

I know the cat of the man that will eat the mouse

I know the owner of the cat that will eat the cake

I see the cat of the woman that will eat the lizard

I see the owner of the cat that will wear the shoes

That is the cat of the woman that will wear the collar

I know the husband of the wife that will push the lawn mower

I see the woman of the man that will push the stroller

I know the husband of the wife that will close the tool box

I know the woman of the man that will close the suitcase

I see the father of the boy that will read the plans

I see the son of the builder that will read the book

That is the father of the boy that will build the house

That is the son of the builder that will build the sand castle

I see the friend of the plumber that will cut the fabric

I know the friend of the tailor that will cut the pipe

That is the friend of the plumber that will repair the sewing machine

That is the friend of the tailor that will repair the sink

I know the father of the child that will use the treadmill

I know the son of the father that will use the tricycle

I see the father of the child that will blow the whistle

I see the son of the father that will blow the bubble

That is the uncle of the boy that will sip the wine

I see the cousin of the hunter that will sip the juice

I know the uncle of the boy that will shoot the fox

I know the cousin of the hunter that will shoot the archery target

That is the owner of the dog that will taste the chocolate

That is the dog of the boy that will taste the dog food

I know the owner of the dog that will use the bed

I know the dog of the boy that will use the doghouse

That is the uncle of the girl that will ride the bull

That is the niece of the cowboy that will ride the carousel

I see the uncle of the girl that will read the newspaper

That is the niece of the cowboy that will read the book

That is the wife of the man that will wear the dress

I know the husband of the woman that will wear the suit

I know the wife of the man that will repair the shoe

I see the husband of the woman that will repair the watch

I know the uncle of the boy that will carry the first aid

I know the nephew of the soldier that will carry the teddy bear

I see the uncle of the boy that will drive the tank

I see the nephew of the soldier that will drive the toy car

LIST OF REFERENCES

LIST OF REFERENCES

Allen, R., & Reber, A. S. (1980). Very long term memory for tacit knowledge. *Cognition, 8*(2), 175-185.

Allopenna, P. D., Magnuson, J. S., & Tanenhaus, M. K. (1998). Tracking the time course of spoken word recognition using eye movements: Evidence for continuous mapping models. *Journal of memory and language*, *38*(4), 419-439.

Altmann, G. T., & Kamide, Y. (1999). Incremental interpretation at verbs: restricting the domain of subsequent reference. *Cognition, 73*(3), 247-264.

Anderson, J. R., Bothell, D., Byrne, M. D., Douglass, S., Lebiere, C., & Qin, Y. (2004).

An integrated theory of the mind. *Psychological Review, 111*(4), 1036.

Arai, M., Van Gompel, R. P., & Scheepers, C. (2007). Priming ditransitive structures in comprehension. *Cognitive psychology, 54*(3), 218-250.

Atkinson, E., Rigby, I., Shapiro, N., Woo, B., & Akira, O. (2018). Syntatic adaptation effects do not transfer across tasks. *2018 CUNY Sentence on Human Sentence Processing*.

Baayen, R. H. (2008). Analyzing linguistic data: A practical introduction to statistics using R: Cambridge University Press.

Barr, D. J. (2008). Analyzing 'visual world'eyetracking data using multilevel logistic regression. *Journal of Memory and language, 59*(4), 457-474.

Bernolet, S., & Hartsuiker, R. J. (2010). Does verb bias modulate syntactic priming? *Cognition, 114*(3), 455-461. doi:10.1016/j.cognition.2009.11.005

Bock, Dell, G. S., Chang, F., & Onishi, K. H. (2007). Persistent structural priming from language comprehension to language production. *Cognition, 104*(3), 437-458. doi:10.1016/j.cognition.2006.07.003

Bock, J. K. (1986). Syntactic persistence in language production. *Cognitive psychology, 18*(3), 355-387.

Bock, J. K., & Griffin, Z. M. (2000). The persistence of structural priming: Transient activation or implicit learning? *Journal of Experimental Psychology: General, 129*(2), 177.

Boersma, P., & Weenink, D. (2016). Praat: doing phonetics by computer [Computer program]. Version 6.0.17, retrieved April 2016 from http://www.praat.org/.

Boland, J. E. (2005). Visual arguments. *Cognition, 95*(3), 237-274. doi:10.1016/j.cognition.2004.01.008

Boland, J. E., de los Santos, G., Carranza, J., & Kaschak, M. (2015). Self-paced reading time as a measure of learning novel constructions. *Poster presented at CUNY 2015 Sentence on Human Sentence Processing*.

Borovsky, A., Elman, J. L., & Fernald, A. (2012). Knowing a lot for one's age: Vocabulary skill and not age is associated with anticipatory incremental sentence interpretation in children and adults. *Journal of experimental child psychology, 112*(4), 417-436.

Branigan, H. P., Pickering, M. J., & McLean, J. F. (2005). Priming prepositional-phrase attachment during comprehension. *J Exp Psychol Learn Mem Cogn, 31*(3), 468- 481. doi:10.1037/0278-7393.31.3.468

Branigan, H. P., Pickering, M. J., Stewart, A. J., & McLean, J. F. (2000). Syntactic priming in spoken production: Linguistic and temporal interference. *Memory & Cognition, 28*(8), 1297-1302.

Brennan, S. E., & Hanna, J. E. (2009). Partner-specific adaptation in dialog. *Topics in cognitive science, 1*(2), 274-291.

Brooks, P. J., & Tomasello, M. (1999). How children constrain their argument structure constructions. *Language*, 720-738.

Chang, F. (2008). Implicit learning as a mechanism of language change. *Theoretical Linguistics, 34*(2), 115-122.

Chang, F., Dell, G. S., & Bock, K. (2006). Becoming syntactic. *Psychological Review, 113*(2), 234.

Chang, F., Janciauskas, M., & Fitz, H. (2012). Language adaptation and learning: Getting explicit about implicit learning. *Language and Linguistics Compass, 6*(5), 259-278.

Chen, Q., Xu, X., Tan, D., Zhang, J., & Zhong, Y. (2013). Syntactic priming in Chinese sentence comprehension:

evidence from Event-Related Potentials. *Brain and cognition, 83*(1), 142-152.

Dahan, D., Swingley, D., Tanenhaus, M. K., & Magnuson, J. S. (2000). Linguistic gender and spoken-word recognition in French. *Journal of Memory and language, 42*(4), 465-480.

Dell, G. S., & Chang, F. (2014). The P-chain: Relating sentence production and its disorders to comprehension and acquisition. *Phil. Trans. R. Soc. B, 369*(1634), 20120394.

DeLong, K. A., Troyer, M., & Kutas, M. (2014). Pre-processing in sentence comprehension: Sensitivity to likely upcoming meaning and structure. *Language and Linguistics Compass, 8*(12), 631-645.

DeLong, K. A., Urbach, T. P., & Kutas, M. (2005). Probabilistic word pre-activation during language comprehension inferred from electrical brain activity. *Nature neuroscience, 8*(8), 1117-1121.

Dussias, P. E., & Sagarra, N. (2007). The effect of exposure on syntactic parsing in Spanish–English bilinguals. *Bilingualism: Language and Cognition, 10*(1), 101- 116.

Farmer, T. A., Brown, M., & Tanenhaus, M. K. (2013). Prediction, explanation, and the role of generative models in language processing. *Behav Brain Sci, 36*(3), 211- 212. doi:10.1017/S0140525X12002312

Farmer, T. A., Fine, A. B., & Jaeger, T. F. (2011). *Implicit context-specific learning leads to rapid shifts in syntactic expectations.* Paper presented at the Proceedings of the 33rd annual meeting of the Cognitive Science Society.

Federmeier, K. D., & Kutas, M. (1999). A rose by any other name: Long-term memory structure and sentence processing. *Journal of Memory and language, 41*(4), 469- 495.

Ferreira, Bock, K., Wilson, M. P., & Cohen, N. J. (2008). Memory for syntax despite amnesia. *Psychological science, 19*(9), 940-946.

Ferreira, V. S. (2003). The persistence of optional complementizer production: Why saying "that" is not saying "that" at all. *Journal of Memory and language, 48*(2), 379-398.

Ferreira, V. S., & Bock, K. (2006). The functions of structural priming. *Language and Cognitive Processes, 21*(7-8), 1011-1029.

Fine, A. B., & Florian Jaeger, T. (2013). Evidence for implicit learning in syntactic comprehension. *Cognitive science, 37*(3), 578-591.

Fine, A. B., & Florian Jaeger, T. (2013). Evidence for implicit learning in syntactic comprehension. *Cogn Sci, 37*(3), 578-591. doi:10.1111/cogs.12022

Fine, A. B., Jaeger, T. F., Farmer, T. A., & Qian, T. (2013). Rapid Expectation Adaptation during Syntactic Comprehension. *PloS one, 8*(10), e77661. doi:10.1371/journal.pone.0077661

Fraundorf, S. H., & Jaeger, T. F. (2016). Readers generalize adaptation to newly- encountered dialectal structures to other unfamiliar structures. *Journal of Memory and language, 91*, 28-58.

Frazier, L., & Clifton, C. (1996). *Construal*: Mit Press.

Hale, J. (2001). *A probabilistic Earley parser as a psycholinguistic model.* Paper presented at the Proceedings of the second meeting of the North American Chapter of the Association for Computational Linguistics on Language technologies.

Hartsuiker, R. J., Bernolet, S., Schoonbaert, S., Speybroeck, S., & Vanderelst, D. (2008). Syntactic priming persists while the lexical boost decays: Evidence from written and spoken dialogue. *Journal of Memory and language, 58*(2), 214-238.

Henry, N., Hopp, H., & Jackson, C. N. (2017). Cue additivity and adaptivity in predictive processing. *Language, Cognition and Neuroscience*, *32*(10), 1229-1249.

Huettig, F., & Janse, E. (2016). Individual differences in working memory and processing speed predict anticipatory spoken language processing in the visual world. *Language, Cognition and Neuroscience, 31*(1), 80-93.

Huettig, F., & Mani, N. (2016). Is prediction necessary to understand language? Probably not. Language, Cognition and Neuroscience, 31(1), 19-31.

Huettig, F., Rommers, J., & Meyer, A. S. (2011). Using the visual world paradigm to study language processing: a review and critical evaluation. *Acta Psychol (Amst), 137*(2), 151-171. doi:10.1016/j.actpsy.2010.11.003

Hwang, H., Lieberman, M., Goad, H., & White, L. (2011). Syntactic ambiguity resolution: Effects of prosodic breaks and prosodic length.

Jaeger, T. F., & Snider, N. E. (2008). *Implicit learning and syntactic persistence: Surprisal and cumulativity.* Paper presented at the Proceedings of the 30th annual conference of the cognitive science society.

Jaeger, T. F., & Snider, N. E. (2013). Alignment as a consequence of expectation adaptation: syntactic priming is affected by the prime's prediction error given both prior and recent experience. *Cognition, 127*(1), 57-83. doi:10.1016/j.cognition.2012.10.013

Kaan, E. (2014). Predictive sentence processing in L2 and L1: What is different? Linguistic Approaches to Bilingualism, 4(2), 257-282.

Kamide, Y. (2012). Learning individual talkers' structural preferences. *Cognition, 124*(1), 66-71.

Kamide, Y., Altmann, G. T., & Haywood, S. L. (2003). The time-course of prediction in incremental sentence processing: Evidence from anticipatory eye movements. *Journal of Memory and language, 49*(1), 133-156.

Kaschak, M. P. (2006). What this construction needs is generalized. *Mem Cognit, 34*(2), 368-379.

Kaschak, M. P., & Glenberg, A. M. (2004). This construction needs learned. *Journal of Experimental Psychology: General, 133*(3), 450.

Kaschak, M. P., Kutta, T. J., & Jones, J. L. (2011). Structural priming as implicit learning: Cumulative priming effects and individual differences. *Psychonomic bulletin & review, 18*(6), 1133-1139.

Kim, C. S., Carbary, K. M., & Tanenhaus, M. K. (2014). Syntactic priming without lexical overlap in reading comprehension. *Language and Speech, 57*(2), 181-195.

Kleinschmidt, D. F., Fine, A. B., & Jaeger, T. F. (2012). *A belief-updating model of adaptation and cue combination in syntactic comprehension.* Paper presented at the Proceedings of the Annual Meeting of the Cognitive Science Society.

Kleinschmidt, D. F., & Jaeger, T. F. (2015). Robust speech perception: recognize the familiar, generalize to the similar, and adapt to the novel. *Psychological Review, 122*(2), 148.

Konopka, A. E., & Bock, J. K. (2005). Helping syntax out: How much do words do? Paper presented at the the 18th CUNY Human Sentence Processing Conference [CUNY 2005].

Kraljic, T., Samuel, A. G., & Brennan, S. E. (2008). First impressions and last resorts: How listeners adjust to speaker variability. *Psychological science, 19*(4), 332- 338.

Kroczek, L. O., & Gunter, T. C. (2017). Communicative predictions can overrule linguistic priors. *Scientific reports, 7*(1), 17581.

Kuperberg, G. R., & Jaeger, T. F. (2016). What do we mean by prediction in language comprehension? *Language, Cognition and Neuroscience, 31*(1), 32-59.

Kutas, M., & Federmeier, K. D. (2000). Electrophysiology reveals semantic memory use in language comprehension. *Trends in cognitive sciences, 4*(12), 463-470.

Kutas, M., & Federmeier, K. D. (2011). Thirty years and counting: finding meaning in the N400 component of the event-related brain potential (ERP). *Annual review of psychology, 62*, 621-647.

Kuznetsova A, Brockhoff PB and Christensen RHB (2017). "lmerTest Package: Tests in Linear Mixed Effects Models." *Journal of Statistical Software*, 82(13), pp. 1–26. doi: 10.18637/jss.v082.i13.

Laszlo, S., & Federmeier, K. D. (2009). A beautiful day in the neighborhood: An event- related potential study of lexical relationships and prediction in context. *Journal of Memory and language, 61*(3), 326-338.

Ledoux, K., Traxler, M. J., & Swaab, T. Y. (2007). Syntactic priming in comprehension: Evidence from event-related potentials. *Psychological science, 18*(2), 135-143.

Levelt, W. J., & Kelter, S. (1982). Surface form and memory in question answering. Cognitive psychology, 14(1), 78-106.

Levy, R. (2008). Expectation-based syntactic comprehension. *Cognition, 106*(3), 1126-1177.

Liu, L., Burchill, Z., Tanenhaus, M. K., & Jaeger, T. F. (2017). *Failure to replicate talker- specific syntactic adaptation*.

Mani, N., & Huettig, F. (2012). Prediction during language processing is a piece of cake—But only for skilled producers. *Journal of Experimental Psychology: Human Perception and Performance, 38*(4), 843.

Marian, V., Blumenfeld, H. K., & Kaushanskaya, M. (2007). The Language Experience and Proficiency Questionnaire (LEAP-Q): Assessing language profiles in bilinguals and multilinguals. *Journal of Speech, Language, and Hearing Research, 50*(4), 940-967.

Nakamura, C., Arai, M., & Mazuka, R. (2012). Immediate use of prosody and context in predicting a syntactic structure. *Cognition, 125*(2), 317-323.

Nieuwland, M., Politzer-Ahles, S., Heyselaar, E., Segaert, K., Darley, E., Kazanina, N., .. . Ito, A. (2017). Limits on prediction in language comprehension: A multi-lab failure to replicate evidence for probabilistic pre-activation of phonology. *BioRxiv*, 111807.

Pickering, M. J., & Branigan, H. P. (1998). The representation of verbs: Evidence from syntactic priming in language production. *Journal of Memory and language, 39*(4), 633-651.

Pickering, M. J., & Ferreira, V. S. (2008). Structural priming: a critical review. Psychological bulletin, 134(3), 427.

Pickering, M. J., & Garrod, S. (2007). Do people use language production to make predictions during comprehension? *Trends in cognitive sciences, 11*(3), 105-110.

Pickering, M. J., McLean, J. F., & Branigan, H. P. (2013). Persistent structural priming and frequency effects during comprehension. *Journal of Experimental Psychology: Learning, Memory, and Cognition, 39*(3), 890.

Pickering., & Branigan. (1998). The representation of verbs: Evidence from syntactic priming in language production. *Journal of Memory and language, 39*(4), 633- 651.

Porretta V, K. A., van Rij J and Järvikivi J. (2017). "VWPre: Tools for Preprocessing Visual World Data." R package version 1.0.1.

R Core Team. (2016). R: A language and environment for statistical computing. Foundation for Statistical Computing, Vienna, Austria. URL https://www.r- project.org/.

Reitter, D., Keller, F., & Moore, J. D. (2011). A computational cognitive model of syntactic priming. *Cognitive science, 35*(4), 587-637.

Reitter, D., & Moore, J. D. (2014). Alignment and task success in spoken dialogue. Journal of Memory and language, 76, 29-46.

Reitter, D., Moore, J. D., & Keller, F. (2006). Priming of syntactic rules in task-oriented dialogue and spontaneous conversation. Paper presented at the 28th Annual Conference of the Cognitive Science Society.

Ryskin, R. A., Qi, Z., Duff, M. C., & Brown-Schmidt, S. (2016). *Constraints on adaptation to syntactic variability between and within speakers*. Paper presented at the 29th Annual CUNY Conference on Human Sentence Processing, University of Florida, Gainesville, FL.

Ryskin, R. A., Qi, Z., Duff, M. C., & Brown-Schmidt, S. (2017). *Syntactic variability between and within speakers: When to adapt, when to generalize?* Paper presented at the 30th Annual CUNY Conference on Human Sentence Processing, MIT, Cambridge, MA.

Savage, C., Lieven, E., Theakston, A., & Tomasello, M. (2003). Testing the abstractness of children's linguistic representations: Lexical and structural priming of syntactic constructions in young children. *Developmental Science, 6*(5), 557-567.

Scheepers, C. (2003). Syntactic priming of relative clause attachments: persistence of structural configuration in sentence production. *Cognition, 89*(3), 179-205.

Schenkein, J. (1980). A taxonomy for repeating action sequences in natural conversation. *Language production, 1*, 21-47.

Smith, N. J., & Levy, R. (2008). *Optimal processing times in reading: a formal model and empirical investigation.* Paper presented at the Proceedings of the Annual Meeting of the Cognitive Science Society.

Steedman, M. (1999). Connectionist sentence processing in perspective. *Cognitive science, 23*(4), 615-634.

Szewczyk, J. M., & Schriefers, H. (2013). Prediction in language comprehension beyond specific words: An ERP study on sentence comprehension in Polish. *Journal of Memory and language, 68*(4), 297-314.

Thothathiri, M., & Snedeker, J. (2008). Give and take: Syntactic priming during spoken language comprehension. *Cognition, 108*(1), 51-68.

Tomasello, M. (2007). Cooperation and communication in the 2nd year of life. *Child Development Perspectives, 1*(1), 8-12.

Tooley, K. M., & Bock, K. (2014). On the parity of structural persistence in language production and comprehension. *Cognition, 132*(2), 101-136. doi:10.1016/j.cognition.2014.04.002

Tooley, K. M., & Traxler, M. J. (2010). Syntactic priming effects in comprehension: A critical review. *Language and Linguistics Compass, 4*(10), 925-937.

Tooley, K. M., & Traxler, M. J. (2018). Implicit learning of structure occurs in parallel with lexically-mediated syntactic priming effects in sentence comprehension. *Journal of Memory and language, 98*, 59-76.

Tooley, K. M., Traxler, M. J., & Swaab, T. Y. (2009). Electrophysiological and behavioral evidence of syntactic priming in sentence comprehension. *Journal of Experimental Psychology: Learning, Memory, and Cognition, 35*(1), 19.

Traxler, M. J. (2008). Lexically independent priming in online sentence comprehension. Psychonomic bulletin & review, 15(1), 149-155.

Van Berkum, J. J., Brown, C. M., Zwitserlood, P., Kooijman, V., & Hagoort, P. (2005). Anticipating upcoming words in discourse: evidence from ERPs and reading times. *Journal of Experimental Psychology: Learning, Memory, and Cognition, 31*(3), 443.

Wei, H., Dong, Y., Boland, J. E., & Yuan, F. (2016). Structural Priming and Frequency Effects Interact in Chinese Sentence Comprehension. *Front Psychol, 7*, 45.

Xie, X., Earle, F. S., & Myers, E. B. (2018). Sleep facilitates generalisation of accent adaptation to a new talker. *Language, Cognition and Neuroscience, 33*(2), 196- 210

Unlocking the Power of Adaptation

How Our Minds Shape Language to Fit the Unexpected

발행일 | 2024년 1월 10일

지은이 | 천은진
펴낸이 | 마형민
기　획 | 임수안
편　집 | 김현주
펴낸곳 | (주)페스트북
주　소 | 경기도 안양시 안양판교로 20
홈페이지 | festbook.co.kr

© Eunjin Chun 2023

저작권법에 의해 보호를 받는 저작물이므로 무단 전재와 무단 복제를 금합니다.
ISBN 979-11-6929-434-8 03700
값 19,500원

* (주)페스트북은 '작가중심주의'를 고수합니다. 누구나 인생의 새로운 챕터를 쓰도록 돕습니다. Creative@festbook.co.kr로 자신만의 목소리를 보내주세요.